THE ELEMEN

Stuart Holroyd has w... ...any .... the years since one of his plays in the 1950s caused him to be regarded as one of the 'Angry Young Men'. Having established and run a school of languages for twenty years, he now lives in France where he writes and teaches.

The *Elements Of* is a series designed to present high quality introductions to a broad range of essential subjects.

The books are commissioned specifically from experts in their fields. They provide readable and often unique views of the various topics covered, and are therefore of interest both to those who have some knowledge of the subject, as well as those who are approaching it for the first time.

Many of these concise yet comprehensive books have practical suggestions and exercises which allow personal experience as well as theoretical understanding, and offer a valuable source of information on many important themes.

In the same series

the elements of

gnosticism

stuart holroyd

Shaftesbury, Dorset • Rockport • Massachusetts • Melbourne, Australia

© Element Books Limited, 1994
Text © Stuart Holroyd 1994

First published in Great Britain in 1994 by
Element Books Limited
Shaftesbury, Dorset SP7 8BP

Published in the USA in 1994 by
Element Books, Inc.
PO Box 830, Rockport, MA 01966

Published in Australia in 1994 by
Element Books and
distributed by Penguin Books Australia Limited
487 Maroondah Highway, Ringwood,
Victoria 3134

Reprinted March and November 1994

Reissued 1997

Cover design by Max Fairbrother
Typeset by The Electronic Book Factory Ltd, Fife, Scotland
Printed and bound in Great Britain by
Biddles Ltd, Guildford & King's Lynn

British Library Cataloguing in Publication
data available

Library of Congress Cataloging in Publication
data available

ISBN 1–86204–146–6

CONTENTS

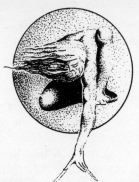

1 · GNOSTICISM ANCIENT AND MODERN

Religions agree that man and the world are imperfect. Where they differ is in explaining why they are so, and in what they propose should be done about it.

Generally speaking, man is held to blame for the situation. Religious myths suggest that there was a time (and fantasy fictions still sometimes would have us imagine that there are places in the world or the universe) of harmony, peace and perfection; with man, God and nature coexisting in blissful symbiosis. It is always man who disrupts and spoils the idyllic state, either from within the system by eating forbidden fruit or otherwise asserting his independent free will, or from outside by infiltrating it and bringing in his wake disorder, disease, death, greed and violence. The myths and fantasy fictions are, of course, products of the human imagination, and when the human imagination dwells on questions of morality and culpability it generally levels the accusing finger at its own kind, either in admonition or as the expression of a deep-rooted sense of individual and collective guilt.

There is, however, an alternative view, namely that the world was imperfect from the start, that the blame lies not with man, but with God, the Creator. Readers who find this idea blasphemous, preposterous or perverse might as well

1

close this book forthwith. Those who find it at least interesting and possibly plausible might be about to find out that they are Gnostics at heart.

Although one rarely hears anyone profess to being a Gnostic today, as they might profess to being a Christian, a Hindu or a Buddhist, it would be wrong to infer that Gnosticism is of historical interest only, that it was an aberrant school of Western spiritual philosophy which flourished in the early centuries of the Christian era and then lost its vitality and appeal, surviving only as a minority cult of specialist scholarly interest. This is how it has been represented by its enemies, but its friends have included writers and thinkers acknowledged as some of the greatest of Western culture: Voltaire, Goethe, Blake, Melville, Yeats, Jung, Hesse, to mention just a few from relatively recent times.

There is, in fact, a substantial corpus of modern gnostic literature. The literary-philosophical school of Existentialism had many affinities with classical Gnosticism. Far from being the exclusive preserve of scholars, Gnosticism has proved to have enduring vitality and appeal. Its appeal is to the psyche, the unconscious, where all the great myths and the truths they embody originate and resonate. It is said that the Devil has all the best tunes, and if we are to believe the orthodox Christian Church, Gnosticism was the work of the Devil.

Its tunes are many and varied, a repertoire, unconstrained by dogma, of variations on themes that the human imagination, human aspirations, and human self-awareness may respond to as embodying truths more profound, or suggesting life possibilities more challenging, than those offered by orthodox religion.

In the second century Bishop Irenaeus of Lyon castigated the Gnostics for their literary fecundity, sneering that they were capable of producing a new gospel every day. His implication was that the copiousness and variety of gnostic literature made preposterous any claim to truth, which to his mind was unequivocally enshrined in the orthodox canon and dogma. Orthodox Christianity insisted on the literal truth of its teaching, and of the historical drama of Jesus Christ's ministry, miracles, crucifixion and resurrection. It had no tolerance of concepts of symbolic or psychological truth, or of heterodox speculations about creation, the cosmos, God, human origins and destiny. There are still literalists and fundamentalists in the Christian Church today, but two millennia of social, scientific and philosophical development have perforce changed man's views of the cosmos, the world and himself. There is no casuistry that can reconcile these changes with religious dogmatic literalism, so the fundamentalists and literalists, however vociferous they may be, are a minority. There are even, among thinking Christians, those who have suggested that their religion might gain a new lease of life by incorporating some aspects of Gnosticism.

Bishop Irenaeus would be appalled that the old enemy, the 'heresy of heresies', should still be challenging and subverting the Faith that he and so many other martyrs died for. But the world has changed. The Faithful have not been conspicuous in their spirituality or exemplary morals these two millennia, and today a person disposed to seek the religious life is less likely to do so through acquiescence to dogma and authority than through some spiritual discipline which might plausibly contribute to the betterment of the individual soul and of the world.

Many people over recent years have turned to the Eastern religions to embrace such a discipline. Most of these probably have not realised that in Gnosticism they had an alternative closer to home, in the sense that it has been a kind of sub-plot in the history of Western culture.

Gnostic teachers and philosophers were individualists who produced their own literary and speculative works without having to subscribe to any particular set of beliefs. In later chapters we shall consider some of the major schools of gnostic thought and the main literarary texts; but obviously if the term Gnostic means anything, the people to whom it applies must have had some things in common, and we must at this stage specify these common elements or ideas. The idea that the world was the work of an incompetent or malevolent deity was one.

3

THE RESPONSIBILITY OF GOD FOR THE FLAWED CREATION

Stated thus baldly, it seems a merely perverse idea, or an attempt to exonerate human iniquity by putting the blame on God. But the gnostic argument is not so maladroit. It maintains that the true God is beyond the created universe and quite alien to it. This transcendent God does not, and never did, act, in the sense of willing something and bringing it about. To begin to understand Gnosticism we have to substitute the idea of divine emanation, or 'bringing forth', for the idea of divine action. There are many variations of the basic gnostic creation myth, as we shall see in due course, and the following brief summary should be regarded as typical rather than as fundamental and general.

In the beginning there existed only the transcendent God, a male principle that existed for eternities in repose with a female principle, the Ennoia (Thought), until there emanated or was brought forth from their union the two archetypes Mind (male) and Truth (female). In turn these principles emanated others, in male – female pairs to the total of thirty, known as Aeons, who collectively constituted the divine realm, known as the Pleroma, or Fullness. Of all the Aeons only the first, Mind, knew and comprehended the greatness of the Father and could behold him, but the last and youngest Aeon, Sophia (Wisdom), became possessed of a passion to do so, and out of the agony of this passion and without the knowledge or consent of her male counterpart, she projected from her own being a flawed emanation.

This abortion, the 'Demiurge', was the creator of the material cosmos and imagined himself to be the absolute God. The cosmos that he created consisted of a number of spheres, each of which is ruled over by one of the lower powers, the Archons, who collectively govern man's world, the earth, which is the lowest of the spheres of the degenerate creation.

DUALISM AND ANTITHESES

Gnostic theology, cosmology and general philosophy espouse a radical dualism, which is aptly expressed by a symbolism of light and darkness. The divine realm is the realm of light, and the Aeons are Beings of light, in contradistinction to the darkness of the cosmic spheres and their rulers, the Archons. Good and evil, spirit and matter, knowledge and ignorance, are other antitheses correlated with the fundamental one of light and darkness. The gnostic verdict on the world is that it is the darkest dungeon of creation, the innermost of the cosmic spheres, where matter, evil and ignorance irredeemably prevail.

Man's nature, too, is dual, consisting of a perishable physical component and a spiritual component which is a fragment of the divine substance, or, to extend the light symbolism, a 'divine spark'. Man is generally ignorant of the spark of divinity that resides in him, and the Archons seek to keep him ignorant by encouraging and gratifying the physical appetites and passions of the 'natural' man. Some Gnostics held that man was created for the express purpose of entrapping the divine spark, for if ever the divine substance is totally gathered into itself again the flawed cosmic creation, the domain of the Archons, will come to an end. When the divine spark is released from its corporeal prison by death, it will aspire to be reunited with the divine substance, but to attain reunion it must undertake a hazardous journey, traversing the spheres where the ever-vigilant Archons lie in wait to frustrate its efforts and to hurl it back, reincarnate, into the toils and bondage of the physical world.

Unawareness and ignorance keep man in thrall to the Archons, it is knowledge (gnosis) alone that can liberate him: knowledge of the transcendent God and of the divinity within, and also knowledge of the way to combat or outwit the Archons and enable the soul to achieve the reunion it yearns for. This saving knowledge cannot be discovered in the world, the realm of darkness. It must come from the realm of light, vouchsafed either by revelation (or illumination) or brought by a messenger, a transcendent saviour. In some gnostic schools the saviour bears the name Christos, or Jesus, but there is a fundamental difference from Christian belief in that the gnostic Christ brings salvation not from sin but from ignorance, offers not redemption but the knowledge that

5

redeems, and demands not belief and contrition but spiritual effort and diligence.

There is an obvious elitism implicit in this. To be awakened to the existence of the divine spark within is in itself to be set apart from the majority of mankind, and actually to possess the gnosis is to attain a rare spiritual distinction. Furthermore, the gnostic contempt for the material and physical world can easily be extended to contempt for human beings who do not see anything intrinsically wrong with the world, and the contempt for the Creator can result in the repudiation of moral principles and prohibitions and the assumption of a status above the law, where anything is permissible.

Both elitism and nihilism are possible consequences of the gnostic world–view, as the Church Fathers never tired of pointing out, but the historical record of gnostic transgression of moral law and the perpetration of crimes against humanity is scant indeed in comparison with the record of the enemies and suppressors of Gnosticism.

GNOSTICISM IN THE MODERN WORLD

Some reasons for the perennial appeal and contemporary relevance of Gnosticism may be suggested on the basis of this sketch of the core ideas.

First, it offers a dramatic account of creation and a view of the created world which may be novel and startling, but which corresponds with the way we are often disposed to see it: as a God-forsaken mess.

Secondly, its emphasis on dualism and the struggle between the physical and spiritual components of human nature agrees with our sense and experience of psychic turbulence and affords us a theoretical framework to help us comprehend and resolve it.

Thirdly, its teachings have a psychological relevance and appeal which supersedes any question of their literal truth. No Gnostic ever sought to coerce belief, for belief is not the way to gnosis. Truth is not manifest and accessible, it is covert and has to be diligently sought out. Gnostic literature assists the process of seeking, which is simultaneously a process of psychic self-exploration and growth. One does not have to believe that the Archons exist in the celestial spheres to understand that they exist and work their mischief in one's own psyche.

Fourthly, it is an established part of Western culture, and strange though its concepts may be they are not alien and exotic. As Westerners with a Christian cultural background, no longer intimidated by charges of heresy, we may find Gnosticism at once familiar enough to be accessible, and intellectually and spiritually challenging enough to engage our interest and efforts.

GNOSTICISM IN HISTORY

Let us now turn to the historical perspective and consider where and when Gnosticism originated and flourished and who the Gnostics were. There has been a good deal of scholarly debate over the question of whether it was merely a Christian heresy, or whether a pre-Christian Gnosticism existed. Indisputably, the first two centuries of the Christian era were the heyday of Gnosticism, when the great schools and teachers flourished and a great body of literature was produced.

These were centuries of extraordinary spiritual and philosophical ferment in the eastern Mediterranean area, when ideas and myths that had been in the air for centuries were consolidated by men of religious genius into systems that exercised a profound influence upon the minds and lives of multitudes. The materials that the Gnostics consolidated can be traced back to Iranian, Egyptian, Greek, Babylonian and Jewish sources, with various combinations of these elements brought into the foreground by individual gnostic writers.

The world in which both the Christian and the gnostic ideas evolved was one still dominated by Hellenic culture and the Greek language. This was soon to be superseded by Roman and Latin dominance, and as Christianity became integral with the new western world order, it looked back upon the old Hellenic order as one of benighted paganism and sought to expunge any residues of Hellenism from its world–view. Thus the Church Fathers imputed that Gnosticism was derivative from Greek, and in particular Platonic, philosophy, and indicted it on this count, not only for being derivative but also because any philosophy formulated before the historical events through which the Truth was revealed was manifestly either false or incomplete and irrelevant.

Writers on the origins of Gnosticism have tended either to go along with the Church Fathers' explanation, or to propose an older, oriental provenance.

The question is complicated by the fact that later Greek culture had assimilated large amounts of oriental thought and mythology. Alexander the Great's conquest of the east in the late fourth century BC created an Hellenic empire in which religions and philosophies formerly limited to a local following became more widely dispersed. The process took time, for it was a two-way influence, a blending of two fundamentally different modes of thought and expression; of the rational, conceptualising Greek mind and the symbolising, mythologising oriental mind. However, by the beginning of the Christian era, oriental thought systematized by the Greek mind and expressed in the Greek language was in a position to compete vigorously with the new religion for the minds of men.

From Iran and the Old Persian religion of Mazdaism came the gnostic view of the universe as a moral battleground, where the forces of good and evil, symbolised as light and darkness, contend for supremacy. The idea of evil as a power and a metaphysical principle actively at work in the universe was alien to the Greek mind, which typically regarded the cosmos as an order governed by divine law and therefore by definition intrinsically good. Iranian theological dualism offered an alternative to the rational Greek view of the universe, which gnostic writers adopted as a fundamental principle of their systems.

Babylon was another source. There the old religion identified deities with the stars and planets, and developed a complex system of specifying how cosmic powers governed terrestrial events and human lives. This was the origin of astrology, which became widely dispersed and popular in the later Greek culture. Gnostic writers took over the concept, but gave it their own characteristic reinterpretation, making cosmic governance a tyrannical imposition upon the spirit and transforming the astral deities into the anti-divine Archons.

Egyptian religion, too, had a contribution to make. Its *Book of the Dead* tells of the perils of the soul as it makes its progress through the Underworld after death, and how its salvation depends upon knowing the appropriate responses to make to each of the several inquisitor gods before whom it must pass. In Gnosticism the descent of the soul becomes an ascent, and its inquisitors are more malevolent than their Egyptian counterparts, but likewise it is knowledge that is the key to salvation; as, indeed, it was in the Mystery cults of the old Greek religion, the Orphic, Chaldean, Dionysian and Eleusinian. It was the Christian concept of salvation by faith that was the novelty, rather than the concept of the *gnosis*. The ancient religions had always been based on the idea that religion was concerned with knowing, that there were mysteries that man might be initiated into or attain understanding of, and that the individual soul benefited from that initiation or understanding. The idea of *gnosis*, of salvation by knowledge, was in fact the least original of the Gnostics' ideas, and it was only because the Church Fathers perceived it as a particularly pernicious challenge to their orthodox salvationist creed that it was given such prominence in their attacks.

To trace the sources of some of the fundamental ideas of Gnosticism is to raise the question whether it was in fact anything more than a syncretic religious philosophy, a system cobbled together out of components of other systems which were sometimes given a new twist or novel interpretation.

Some of its denigrators have argued along this line, but if it had been merely a synthesis of diverse traditions and ideas with some intellectually exciting or interesting innovations its appeal would have been superficial and ephemeral. It would have lacked the emotional and spiritual element without which conceptual systems are lifeless and barren. The Gnostics were not eclecticists, they were consolidators and transmitters of a spiritual philosophy which came down from ancient times. No matter if the component traditions were

9

diverse: they were not crudely cobbled together but finely and passionately blended, and their spirit was not destroyed in the process but enhanced by it.

It is difficult for us today to imagine the spiritual and intellectual ferment of the eastern Mediterranean in those first two centuries. The colossus that arose out of the melée tends to obscure the view. The profusion of creeds, cults, visionaries, philosophers, teachers, schools, sects, communities, priesthoods, magicians, holy men and 'saviours' was bewildering. Traditions, ideas, schools of thought influenced each other, often clashed, sometimes blended. People happily died, and others righteously slaughtered, for their beliefs. The intellectual and spiritual hunger of people was prodigious, and prodigiously catered to. It is in this context that we must place the emergence and development of Gnosticism.

The surviving original gnostic literature must be a small fraction of what was produced in that creative heyday, and for the most part that fraction has come down to us in fragmentary form.

When the great library at Alexandria was ransacked by Christian fanatics in 387, and what was left of it incinerated by the Mohammedans in 641, an inestimable wealth of gnostic literature must have been destroyed. Until the nineteenth century the main source of knowledge of Gnosticism was, ironically, in the writings of the Church Fathers, who in their refutations summarised gnostic texts and often quoted at length from them. In the nineteenth and present centuries a number of original gnostic texts came to light, the most sensational find being an entire library of fifty-two texts discovered at Nag Hammadi in Upper Egypt in 1946. These, scholars later ascertained, had belonged to an ascetic Christian community which, fearing discovery by the ecclesiastical authorities and the consequences of being charged with heresy, had sealed up their forbidden library in a large jar and buried it in the sand beneath a cliff near their monastery in about the year 360.

There must have existed many such communities and collections of texts, but the Church Militant was ruthless and thorough in its suppression of subversive ideas and people who held or propounded them. It has taken patient and dedicated scholarship to build up a coherent picture of the teachings and teachers that the early Church Fathers found so threatening, and in many ways the picture that has emerged justifies their fears. Gnosticism was fundamentally incompatible with an institutionalized, proselytizing, authoritarian mass religion, and if the 'Good News' of salvation through Jesus was to be the foundation stone of the new religion, the Gnostics, with their individualism, their emphasis on the arduousness of the spiritual journey, and their own ideas about who Jesus was and what he taught and did, were bad news indeed. They, and their works, had to go.

2 · GNOSTICISM AND CHRISTIANITY

For Christians, the most celebrated, or rather notorious, of the Gnostics was Simon Magus. They could read about him in the New Testament *Acts of the Apostles*, although the narrative there is brief and, naturally, casts him in an unfavourable light. It tells how, when the apostle Philip went to preach in Samaria, he found the people in thrall to the teachings of Simon, who claimed to be the Messiah, and who was accompanied in his ministry by a woman named Helena whom he had found in a brothel in Tyre and who was now redeemed by him, as others would be redeemed who followed him. If this dubious partnership were not sufficient to discredit Simon, the account further relates how, envying the genuine spiritual power of Philip, he tried to bribe the apostle to divulge the secret of it – thus giving his name to the sin of 'simony', or seeking to buy power.

The biblical story is in itself of little interest or importance, except in so far as it acknowledges the challenge of the gnostic teachings as early as the apostolic era. However, later Christian writers accorded Simon more importance, if not respect, regarding him as the father of all heresy and indicating that there existed an extensive Simonian literature, which may have been his own work or that of a school. Their commentaries on and quotations from this literature do not support the implications of the story in the *Acts* that Simon was a charlatan, a braggart, a mere wonder-worker, and a lecher to boot. They indicate rather that he was a subtle and coherent gnostic teacher with a dramatic flair for getting his message across.

The Simonian version of the gnostic creation myth held that the female principle, the Ennoia, having generated the Demiurge (creator of the material cosmos), was dragged down from the highest heaven by the powers that were her progeny into the physical world, where

> she suffered all manner of abuse from them, that she might not return upward to her Father, and this went so far that she was even enclosed in human flesh and migrated for centuries as from vessel to vessel into different female bodies. And since all the Powers contended for her possession, strife and warfare raged among the nations wherever she appeared . . . Migrating from body to body, she at last became a whore in a brothel.[6]

Which, of course, is where Simon picked her up, according to the *Acts*. So his Helena was not merely a whore he had rescued, she was the Ennoia, the female emanation and consort of the highest God, the divine principle imprisoned in matter, the spirit trapped and degraded in the flesh. Simon himself claimed to be that highest God incarnate, who

> came, first to raise her up and release her from her bonds, and then to bring salvation to all men through knowledge of him. For since the angels ruled the world evilly, because each of them coveted the mastery, he has come to set things right, and has descended, transforming and assimilating himself to the virtues and powers of the angels, so that eventually among men he appeared as a man, though he was not one, and was thought to have suffered in Judaea, though he did not suffer.[6]

According to one of the Church Fathers, what he taught was

13

The prophets uttered their prophesies inspired by the angels that made the world; wherefore those who placed their hope in himself and his Helena need no longer heed them and might freely do what they liked. For only by his grace men were saved, not by righteous deeds. For works are not in their nature good or bad, but by external dispensation: the angels who made the world decreed them as such, by precepts of this kind to bring man into servitude. Wherefore he promised that the world should be dissolved and that his own should be liberated from the dominion of those who made the world.[6]

It would appear that the gnostic teaching was fairly fully and subtly developed by Simon's day. The creation myth and the cosmogony were later more elaborated upon by the Aeonology and the role played by Sophia, but the basic components were already in place: the distinction between the transcendent God and the creator of the physical cosmos, the conjunction of male and female principles in the divinity, the drama of the fall, capture and imprisonment of the spirit and the descent of the saviour-God through the spheres, the doctrine of reincarnation, the contempt for the physical world and for the precepts and principles laid down to govern man's conduct within it. These were the fundamental themes of Gnosticism in general. Elements that were specific to the Simonian teaching were the personification of the female divinity in the whore Helena, Simon's claim to be God the Father and to have incarnated previously as God the Son in the figure of Jesus, and the identification of the evil creator with the God of the Jews. This latter point was reported by another of the Church Fathers who wrote about Simon, attributing to him a thesis which criticised the Old Testament God and the serpent legend in *Genesis*. As we shall see later, other gnostic writers developed these themes.

The only records we have of Simon's life and teachings are by Christian writers, and therefore are highly prejudiced. He is derided as a mere magician and showman. There is a tradition that he went to Rome, where he held disputations with the apostle Peter. The story goes that he sought to demonstrate his powers by attempting to fly (or according to one source to ascend back to heaven), but was, as it were, shot down by a well-aimed prayer of Peter's. Not all that is reported of him is as crassly polemical as this, however. There is one particular saying reported of him that rings remarkably true. It is addressed to Peter, and goes:

> Thou indeed as one stupefied continually stoppest thy ears that they may not be polluted by blasphemy and takest to flight, finding nothing to reply; and the unthinking people assenting unto thee will yet approve thee as one teaching what is familiar to them: but me they will execrate, as one who professes novel and unheard-of things.[6]

The story in the *Acts* would have us believe that Simon was eventually converted and baptised, and it is rather curious that the Church Fathers who wrote about him did not substantiate the canonical text. He clearly remained unrepentant and contentious to the end, formidable in dispute and in his conviction. The story of his conversion might go down with the credulous masses of the faithful, but for learned and intelligent Christians the 'father of all heresies' could not be so lightly dismissed. The 'novel and unheard-of things' that he taught, the gnostic religion in other words, had to be taken seriously as a threat and rival to the 'true Faith', and had to be refuted intellectually as well as derided. From what orthodox Christians wrote about Simon Magus one gains the impression that the threat they perceived and the enemy they fought was without, not in their own midst. With his whore in tow and his egregious claims he was a parody saviour, a rival, maybe, but a manifestly feeble one. But the gnostic heresy was not so easily distanced and disposed of; there were many Gnostics who considered themselves to be perfectly good Christians.

THE ESTABLISHMENT OF THE CHURCH

We must bear in mind that it took a long time to establish what being a Christian entailed, both by way of conduct and in matters of belief. The scriptural canon was not established until the turn of the second century, and not until the year 325 were the strict tenets of the Christian creed laid down by the Council of Nicea. Until then precisely what constituted orthodoxy was by no means clear. The first verse of Luke's gospel and the last verse of John's tell us that there were many other non-canonical gospels. The four that were incorporated in the New Testament were alleged to derive their authority from being the earliest, and written either by apostles themselves (Matthew and John) or their followers (Mark and Luke). But there were also gospels attributed to the apostles Peter, Philip and Thomas, and to Mary Magdalene, and although these attributions may well be fictitious there is nothing but the Church's say-so to prove that the canonical gospels were not likewise.

The synoptic gospels (Matthew, Mark and Luke) are distinguished from the non-canonical gospels by their narrative form: they tell the story of Jesus's life, ministry, death and resurrection, they relate events that allegedly occurred in historical time. Orthodox Christianity took its stand on the literal truth of these events, and required its congregations to profess belief in them without any equivocations regarding their symbolic significance. The non-canonical gospels have little narrative, their content is confined to the teachings of Jesus, his sayings, and his responses to questions put to him by his followers, and many of these are enigmatic or equivocal, for the Jesus of these gospels is the teacher of the *gnosis*, of the knowledge that leads to spiritual growth and enlightenment. Both Mark and Matthew report that Jesus taught his intimates things that he did not attempt to convey to the masses, to whom he spoke only in parables. ('To you it has been given to know the secrets of the kingdom of heaven, but to them it has not been given' [*Matthew* 13:11]). The discovery of the Nag Hammadi library was particularly exciting as some of the material, in particular the *Gospel of Thomas*, might incorporate the lost esoteric teachings of Jesus.

We can understand why the Church Fathers chose the gospels that they did to constitute the canon. They were concerned with establishing a Church, not with fostering

16

people's spiritual growth and enlightenment; with promoting a religion that anyone could understand and practise, not one for a select group of spiritual aspirants and intellectuals. Had not Jesus himself said that there would be a Church, and that the apostle Peter would be the 'rock' upon which it would be founded? They believed so, and since Jesus had not specified how the Church should be constituted and governed, and had said very little about the forms of worship, the Church Fathers took it upon themselves to work out these details. They made the 'rock', Peter, posthumously the first Bishop of Rome, and proposed that his successors in the post constituted an 'apostolic succession' whose authority and access to doctrinal truth was beyond dispute. The Christian message was that all men could be saved, which meant that the Church had to be universal (that is 'catholic'), which in turn implied that both its forms of organization and of worship and ritual should be the same everywhere, and therefore strictly governed by an hierarchical structure of authority. The same applied to doctrine: people must accept authority's view of what was true and relevant; if they were allowed to read and speculate as they liked there could never be any consensus of belief.

GNOSTICS AND THE CHURCH

The Gnostics did not take kindly to authority. There were those among them who repudiated all terrestrial authority on principle, as deriving from the counterfeit God who created and governs the world. For others it was simply irrelevant as no submission to authority could lead to gnosis, and no one who had achieved gnosis would submit to spiritual authority. Within the gnostic schools there were teachers who had followers and disciples, and who even practised rituals of initiation, but they had no vested interest in exercising authority.

In the middle of the second century there were groups of gnostic Christians within the Church who, when they met for worship, would draw lots to ascertain who among them should for the occasion take the role of priest, offer the sacrament, read from the scriptures or deliver the sermon. Such a usurpation and, as they saw it, mockery of clerical authority, was execrated by the orthodox, and in their view it was made even worse by the fact that women stood on an equal footing with men in these Christian communities.

The Gnostics could be charged with being spiritually elitist, but certainly not with being sexist. In this matter the differences between Gnosticism and Christianity go deep. The Church was (and indeed still remains) resolutely patriarchal, vesting authority exclusively in the male and requiring of the female unquestioning obedience and compliance in matters spiritual and doctrinal, while sanctifying her in the role of mother and endowing the stereotype with an exaggerated degree of reverence.

The Gnostics did not so polarize and stereotype gender distinctions, either in doctrine or in practice. Certainly their transcendent God was a Father figure, but he existed in union with a feminine principle, the Ennoia, and the divine realm of the Aeons was constituted of equal male-female pairs.

Although it was the female Aeon, Sophia, whose transgression brought forth the creator of the degenerate cosmos, that creator himself is male, and in several gnostic texts Sophia (whose name means Wisdom) admonishes him for his error and arrogance.

Christian attitudes to the female derived from Judaism. Whether it was Gnosticism's more oriental roots, or that some of the spirit of the earlier era of matriarchy had been carried down in one of the several streams from antiquity that nourished it, the fact is that Gnosticism accorded the female, both metaphysically and in life, more respect and more status than did the Church.

THE CREATION MYTHS

There are two biblical myths of creation. One has it that Eve was created out of Adam's rib, and the other that God said, 'Let us make man in our image, after our likeness . . . and . . . in the image of God he created him; male and female he created them' (*Genesis* 1:26-27). The latter account can be interpreted as meaning that God is dyadic, combining male and female principles, and even if such a reading may be contested at least the account gives the female parity with the male, whereas the 'Adam's rib' version implies a secondary and subordinate status. When gnostic writers refer to the *Genesis* stories it is invariably the male-female parity version that they approve, and from which they develop their own theses. The 'Adam's rib' version, on the other hand, was often referred to by Christian writers when any dispute arose as to the status of the female, whether in the Church or the family.

Furthermore, Eve does not come across very creditably in the Garden of Eden story, being taken in by the blandishments of the serpent and prevailing upon Adam with her female wiles to disobey God and eat the fruit of the tree of knowledge. Gnostic interpretations of the myth, however, turn its ostensible meaning inside out. The serpent is the wisest creature in Paradise, and God's prohibition is motivated by malice and envy, because he does not want man to awaken to knowledge, and moreover his threat of death turns out to be an empty one. One gnostic text relates that:

> Then the Female Spiritual Principle came in the Snake, the Instructor, and it taught them, saying, . . . 'you shall not die, for it was out of jealousy that he said this to you. Rather, your eyes shall open, and you shall become like gods, recognizing evil and good' . . . And the arrogant Ruler cursed the Woman . . . and . . . the Snake.[6]

The God of the Old Testament was indisputably an embarrassment, with his wrath, jealousy, vengeance, tribal zealotry and general bossiness, and one might wonder why the Church Fathers took over the Jewish Bible as canonical scripture along with the chosen literature about Jesus Christ, the Saviour. Clearly they did so because the messianic prophesies in the Old Testament lent credence and authority to their doctrines as to who Jesus was and the significance of his terrestrial career, and also because of the doctrinal need to counterpoint the 'original sin' of Adam with the redemptive sacrifice of Christ, although in acquiring a venerable tradition for the new religion they also acquired a catalogue of the deity's deeds and misdeeds that was difficult to reconcile with the idea of God the Father, the fountainhead of love and justice.

One can understand the appeal and plausibility of the gnostic ideas that the true God was transcendent, not only cosmogonically but also in the sense of being above behaving as humans behaved, jealously or vengefully, and that if there were a god who behaved as some of the scriptures described, he must be a pretender, a sham; and furthermore, if in his ignorance and arrogance he really believed he was supreme and irreproachable, he deserved only contempt.

The Gnostics could be represented as wicked and blasphemous atheists to those who did not think too deeply about the implications of the Old Testament narratives, or were persuaded that God's 'mysterious ways' were beyond their comprehension and judgement, but in fact the two–gods hypothesis of Gnosticism could be regarded as making more sense of the world and of recorded history than Judaeo-Christian monotheism, which, allied with a doctrine of scriptural infallibility, put believers in a position where they had no option but to suspend thought altogether and found their religion on faith; which, of course, was what the Church advocated.

FAITH, PERSECUTION AND MARTYRDOM

Tertullian, who famously declared that he believed the literal truth of Christ's resurrection precisely because it was absurd ('*credo quia absurdum est*'), was a leading opponent of the Gnostics. He attacked them, among other reasons, for exalting reason and intellect above faith, declaring:

> Away with all attempts to produce a mixed Christianity of Stoic, Platonic and dialectic composition! We want no curious disputation after possessing Christ Jesus, no inquiring after enjoying the gospel! With our faith, we desire no further belief.[9]

20

That thought and the critical spirit cannot take one far along the spiritual path, and ultimately have to be dispensed with, is attested by all the great teachers and religious traditions, but the advocacy of unquestioning belief in specific miraculous events in the past, and equally prodigious wonders to come, is something we find emphatically insisted upon only in Christianity and Islam. The soul is not something that has to be awakened, educated, refined, separated from the trammels of the material and physical by spiritual effort in life, but something that can secure its salvation and its joyous posthumous existence in eternity through the simple act of belief.

It is easy to deride those who repudiate reason and exalt faith, but the faithful have a powerful argument in their favour, in that they will die for their beliefs. At the time when the Gnostics and the Church Fathers were disputing their views, thousands of Christians were being slaughtered by the Romans, often in the appallingly cruel circumstances of public spectacles, and were embracing their terrible deaths with extraordinary fortitude, convinced that through martyrdom they earned salvation and eternal life. The apostles Peter and James had themselves been martyred; and there is no doubt that the Church's eventual power and Christianity's appeal were cemented by their endurance of and moral triumph over persecution. One of the criticisms levelled at the Gnostics was that they were not persecuted and put to death like genuine Christians. Tertullian even suggested that the heresy was nothing but a stratagem to exonerate cowardice:

> This among Christians is a time of persecution. When, therefore, the faith is greatly agitated, and the church on fire . . . then the gnostics break out; then the Valentinians creep forth; then all the opponents of martyrdom bubble up.[9]

The slur is not true, and there were Gnostics who suffered martyrdom, but on the whole the Gnostics' attitude was that people who embraced such deaths were lamentably misguided, and the enthusiasm of the Church's leaders' for

21

martyrdom, and their propaganda for it, was an appalling imposition upon their naive and innocent following, particularly when the victims were children. When the propagandists claimed that martyrdom was pleasing to God, who joyously welcomed the souls of Christian martyrs into heaven, the Gnostics asked what kind of god could be pleased by such barbarity and suffering. The argument lent support to their contention that the world was governed by a counterfeit and malevolent god.

The persecuted primitive Church of the second century was to become in the fourth century itself the persecutor, and whereas in the earlier period Gnostics had been able to engage in theological dispute with the orthodox, later they were sought out, excommunicated, and sometimes burnt alive for their heresy.

The Church prevailed and prospered, having learnt from its erstwhile oppressors how to maintain and expand an imperial organization. In the twelfth century its inquisitors were mightily exercised in stamping out resurgent Gnosticism in the Languedoc, which necessitated incinerating thousands of Cathars. That is a story we shall come to in due course.

THE NAG HAMMADI TEXTS

Let us now return to those texts that were buried in the Egyptian desert at the time of the fourth century persecution. Let us see what they tell us about the gnostic Jesus, for this was the main issue of contention between orthodox and gnostic Christians.

It is a moot point whether any of the Nag Hammadi texts contain the actual teachings of the historical Jesus. Although nobody seriously argues that Jesus was a Gnostic, it is certainly conceivable that there were gnostic elements in his teachings that were deliberately excluded from the canonical gospels. We know that it was a common and accepted practice in the second century to ascribe writings to the apostles, and that the apostles Thomas, Philip and John, and also Mary Magdalene, were considered more gnostic than the martyrs Peter and

James. Undoubtedly most of the writings in the library have
to be read as imaginative compositions whose interest for us
lies in what they tell about Gnosticism rather than what they
tell us about Jesus. One text, however, *The Gospel of Thomas*,
stands out, and raises the intriguing question as to whether it
might contain authentic material. Its opening sentence reads:
'These are the secret sayings which the living Jesus spoke,
and which Didymos Judas Thomas wrote down'. There is
nothing equivocal about that, and when we recall Mark's
and Matthew's testimonies that there were secret teachings,
the possibility that these are some of them cannot be rejected
out of hand. Furthermore, scholars have dated *The Gospel
of Thomas* as contemporaneous with, and quite possibly
antecedent to, the composition of the canonical gospels.
Many of the sayings are familiar, but differ slightly from the
New Testament versions, generally by being less eloquently
composed and finished. It would appear that either the *Gospel
of Thomas* derived its material from the same source as the
canonical gospels, or was itself a source.

A gnostic note is struck in the first two sayings:

Whoever finds the interpretation of these sayings will
not experience death.

and:

Let him who seeks continue seeking until he finds. When
he finds, he will become troubled. When he becomes
troubled, he will be astonished, and he will rule over
all.[10]

Interpreting, understanding, seeking and finding, attaining
mastery: these are gnostic prescriptions for salvation. There is
no exhortation to faith. The third saying continues in the same
vein, with the familiar gnostic injunction to self-knowledge:

When you come to know yourselves, then you will
become known, and you will realize that it is you who
are the sons of the living father. But if you will not know

yourselves, you will dwell in poverty and it is you who are that poverty.

In a remarkable saying later in the gospel there is a statement with regard to self-knowledge that any modern psychotherapist might display in his consulting room:

If you bring forth what is within you, what you bring forth will save you. If you do not bring forth what is within you, what you do not bring forth will destroy you.

This suggests that gnosis is not merely understanding, not a passive thing; it is a labour, a bringing forth; the projection and expression of elements of the psyche that must be positively integrated if self-knowledge and wholeness are to be achieved. No wonder the psychologist Carl Jung was fascinated by the Gnostics.

In addition to sayings, The Gospel of Thomas contains some passages of dialogue between Jesus and the disciples, generally in question and answer form, with the disciples putting rather naive questions and Jesus responding suitably enigmatically. This Jesus is not without a sense of humour. To the question whether or not circumcision is beneficial he replies, 'If it were beneficial, their father would beget them already circumcised from their mother'. On one occasion he becomes the questioner, and asks the disciples to compare him with someone and tell him whom they think he is like. Peter answers that he is like 'a righteous angel'. Matthew says he is like a wise philosopher, but Thomas answers, 'Master, my mouth is wholly incapable of saying whom you are like'. To which Jesus replies: 'I am not your master, because you have drunk, you have become intoxicated from the bubbling spring which I have measured out'. The meaning of this latter statement is clarified by a later one: 'He who will drink from my mouth will become like me. I myself shall become he, and the things that are hidden will be revealed to him'. So Thomas has advanced further in the gnosis than the other disciples. Now Jesus takes him aside and tells him three things. When he returns to the others they ask him what he has been told, and he answers: 'If I tell you one of the things which he told me, you will pick up stones and throw them at me; a fire will come out of the stones and burn you up'. The implication is that there are levels of spiritual attainment at which certain things can be known which at lower levels would not be rightly comprehended or would even be destructive.

Like a Zen master, Jesus sometimes answers straight questions with riddles. Asked by the disciples; 'Shall we then, as children, enter the kingdom?' he replies:

> When you make the two one, and when you make the inside like the outside and the outside like the inside, and the above like the below, and when you make the male and the female one and the same, so that the male not be male nor the female female; and when you fashion eyes in place of an eye, and a hand in place of a hand, and a foot in place of a foot, and a likeness in place of a likeness; then you will enter the kingdom.[10]

There was something for them to ponder. One of the disciples' chief concerns is when the kingdom of heaven on earth will come. The New Testament generally gives the impression that this will be an event in historical time, a radical upheaval and regeneration of the terrestrial order, and the disciples in *The Gospel of Thomas* have this temporal expectation. Twice they ask when the kingdom will come, and Jesus answers: 'What you look forward to has already come, but you do not recognize it', and: 'It will not come by waiting for it. It will not be a matter of saying "here it is" or "there it is". Rather, the kingdom of the father is spread upon the earth, and men do not see it.' What this teaching implies is that it is not the world that must change, but human consciousness. This essentially gnostic message found its way into Luke's gospel ('the kingdom of God is within you', Luke 17:21), but there are more statements in the New Testament that encourage expectation of world transformation by divine intervention than by individual spiritual effort.

Of course, Jesus's being in the world is an instance of divine intervention, and this is a point upon which both orthodox and gnostic Christians agreed. The Saviour is a spiritual being incarnate, descended from the kingdom of the Father or, in the gnostic view, from the Aeonic world beyond the degenerate and misruled cosmos, to rescue souls from their terrestrial misery and bondage. *The Gospel of Thomas* does not regale us with a dramatic account of the descent or a sensational allegory of the debasement of the soul, in the manner of Simon Magus, but its Jesus does use characteristic gnostic terminology when he speaks of his dismay at discovering just how far human beings had fallen:

> I took my place in the midst of the world, and I appeared to them in flesh. I found all of them intoxicated; I found none of them thirsty. And my soul became afflicted for the sons of men, because they are blind in their hearts and do not have sight; for empty they came into the world, and empty too they seek to leave the world. But for the moment they are intoxicated.

And he goes on to express typical gnostic contempt for the physical:

> If the flesh came into being because of the spirit, it is a wonder. But if spirit came into being because of the body, it is a wonder of wonders. Indeed, I am amazed at how this great wealth has made its home in this poverty.[10]

No wonder the disciples were puzzled as to who this extraordinary being was, who spoke to them like somebody truly not of this world. They asked, 'Who are you, that you should say such things to us?' He answered, 'You do not know who I am from what I say to you?' They should have learnt not to expect straight answers to such questions, but they persisted with them: 'Show us the place where you are, since it is necessary for us to seek it'. Which brought the reply: 'Whoever has ears to hear, let him hear. There is light within a man of light, and he lights up the whole world. If he does not shine, he is darkness.'

Once again the language and metaphor are typically gnostic,

as they are in a statement formulated like the familiar beati-
tudes, but strikingly different from them in spirit: 'Blessed are
the solitary and elect, for you will find the kingdom. For you
are from it, and to it you will return.'

The meek, the poor, the burdened, the captive and oppressed,
the sick and the maimed, the little children, are not the
beneficiaries of the gnostic Jesus's ministrations. This is not
the merciful Lord who has become flesh and will undergo
the tribulations of the flesh out of compassion for the human
race. This saviour does not go around healing the sick and
restoring vital functions to the disabled. He is, essentially,
the spiritual teacher and guide, the initiator of the elect
into gnosis. Although it is not suggested that the elect are
a divinely chosen spiritual elite, it is clear that the qualify-
ing conditions for embarking upon the quest for gnosis are
pretty stringent, involving a renunciation of the world and of
physical satisfactions of which only a minority of ascetically
disposed individuals would ever be capable. It is true that
ordinary Christians undergoing the rite of baptism renounced
'the world, the flesh and the devil', but what made the self-
elected gnostic Christians different was that they actually did
so, and, acknowledging no rite of confession and exculpation
for backsliding or occasional lapses into human frailty, made
doing so the conditio sine qua non of their religious life.

Undeniably there is something inhuman in Gnosticism,
even anti-human, a repugnance felt and expressed for all
things we associate with being human, which no doubt in part
explains why orthodox Christianity, with its emphasis on the
humanity of Jesus, prevailed. It has to be appreciated, however,
that the orthodox emphasis was a theological outcome of a
process of disputation within the primitive church in which
Gnostics played a prominent part. The central story of the
Passion (suffering) of Jesus, his crucifixion and resurrection,
is so extraordinary, so redolent of myth and mystery, that it is
not surprising there should have been vigorous debate as to
how it should be construed. We know from the testimony of
disinterested contemporary historians, Josephus and Tacitus,
that Jesus was crucified and presumably died on the cross, but
subsequent events, the resurrection, the several appearances

to certain of the disciples, the admonitions and teachings he uttered on these occasions, and the ascension to heaven after forty days, obviously carry a weight of interpretative significance that makes their literal truth questionable; and indeed makes questionable too the need for their literal truth to be dogmatically affirmed; their symbolic and exemplary significance is enough to found a religion upon.

The statement attributed to Simon Magus, that he had previously incarnated in Judaea 'as a man, though he was not one, and was thought to have suffered . . . though he did not suffer', can be related to a view developed by one of the earliest gnostic schools, the Docetae ('Illusionists'), and therefore known as docetism, that the Christ-nature was essentially spiritual and the substantiality of the physical body in which it manifested was illusory. There is a docetic *Apocalypse of Peter* among the Nag Hammadi texts, in which the disciple tells how he saw Jesus 'glad and laughing' on the cross while the nails were being driven into his hands and feet. Jesus explains:

> He whom you saw on the tree, glad and laughing, this is the living Jesus. But this one into whose hands and feet they drive nails is his fleshly part, which is the substitute being put to shame, the one who came into being in his likeness. But look at him and me.

In another gnostic text, the *Acts of John*, the author relates how at the time of the crucifixion he fled to the Mount of Olives, where Jesus appeared to him in a cave, which he 'filled with light', and said:

> To the multitude below, in Jerusalem, I am being crucified and pierced with lances and reeds, and gall and vinegar is given me to drink. To thee now I speak, and hearken to my words. It was I who put it in thy heart to ascend this mount, that thou mightest hear what disciple must learn from Master, and man from God.[10]

Some Gnostics, like the Hindus, the Platonists, and indeed modern physicists, held that the material and physical world is ultimately appearance and illusion, while others stressed its substantiality in order the more contemptuously to deplore the entrapment of the spirit within it. Thus with regard to the crucifixion, some would maintain that it was an event in the world of appearance, witnessed by the deluded and uninitiated (in the *Apocalypse of Peter*, Peter says of the crowd witnessing the crucifixion but not seeing the 'glad and laughing' Jesus, 'Lord, no one is looking at you', and Jesus replies, 'I have told you. Leave the blind alone.'), while others would stress the irrelevance of the sufferings undergone by Jesus on the cross. Both views were anathema to orthodox doctrine, which dwelt upon the acute physical and even mental sufferings ('Lord, why hast Thou forsaken me') that Jesus underwent. It is understandable that a faith, many of whose devotees suffered martyrdom in circumstances even more appalling than those experienced by Jesus, should despise and denigrate any views that denied or mitigated the Saviour's own physical suffering. It is understandable, too, that a salvationist religion packs greater emotional clout by postulating a saviour who suffered and died as a human being in a specific place at a specific time in order to redeem both collective and individual human sin. Nothing in the gnostic teachings drew more fire and wrath from the Church Fathers than what the latter regarded as their prevarications and casu-istries over the truth and relevance of the Passion of Christ. But from an objective point of view, orthodox Christianity not less than Gnosticism is an interpretation of and elaboration upon an attested historical event. The literalness and temporality of the event may be emphasised in the interests of teaching salvationism, or the symbolic relevance of the event may be explored in the interests of developing or teaching a spiritual philosophy. Truth, as Kierkegaard said, is subjectivity.

The other doctrine that has to do with the physicality of Jesus is that of the Resurrection. Orthodoxy took a firm stand on the teaching that Jesus, 'crucified, dead and buried', rose from the grave on the third day *in the flesh*.

The canonical gospels are in fact ambiguous about this. Jesus was seemingly an incorporeal presence when he appeared to Mary Magdalene and forbade her to touch him, and also when he appeared to the two disciples on the road to Emmaus and suddenly vanished after discoursing with them and blessing their bread, but he is a manifestly physical presence when he eats a piece of broiled fish in front of the astonished disciples, and when he urges 'doubting Thomas' to touch his wounds.

To Gnostics, the very idea of Jesus's resurrection in the flesh was not only preposterous but also repugnant, for the flesh essentially belongs to the debased order of creation, and the gnostic quest was to liberate the spirit from it. Those Christian Gnostics who wrote about the resurrection regarded the risen Christ as an incorporeal and spiritual presence, though not with the implication that he was the less real, or merely a vision or hallucination. Indeed, they attributed the most profound and mystical teachings to the resurrected Master, and a substantial body of gnostic literature consists of accounts of posthumous manifestations and teachings. If orthodox Christianity had embraced the gnostic view of the resurrection – which it could well have done since even the canonical gospels suggest it – it would surely have constituted a religion more acceptable to the rational mind, and indeed less repugnant to the sensibilities, for who can contemplate without distaste the idea of the dead rising from their graves en masse in the flesh on the Day of Judgement? Even Stanley Spencer's painting of the event makes one shudder with horror.

So why did the Church Fathers make belief in the bodily death and resurrection of Jesus such a fundamental article of faith? As Elaine Pagels has pointed out, the reason was political. Anybody can claim to have had a spiritual encounter with Christ, and seek to legitimise teachings by attributing them to such an encounter, but if the risen Christ was a physical being, who appeared to and talked with the disciples during the forty day period between the resurrection and his ascension to heaven, these encounters and the teachings that emanated from them carry more authority than any alleged spiritual or visionary encounters – indeed, it may be claimed that they alone carry authority. Besides, the risen Christ was said to have named Peter as his successor, and the status of Peter as the first Bishop of Rome was held to legitimise and sanctify the authority of all his successors in that post, and by extension those lower in the ecclesiastical hierarchy whose authority the Bishop consecrated. Belief in the actual corporeal presence of Christ during those forty days was central to asserting the legitimacy of the ecclesiastical order and authority and to maintaining it for all time. The Church Fathers were nothing if not ingenious.

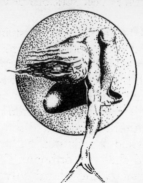

3 · THE MAJOR SCHOOLS OF GNOSTIC THOUGHT

VALENTINUS

Little is known of the man generally acknowledged to have been the greatest of the gnostic teachers. Valentinus was born in Egypt about the year 100, he taught in Rome for about the period 135-160, and then returned to Alexandria, where he died in about 180. He was said to have been a prolific writer of philosophy and poetry, but the only fragments of his work that survive are those quoted in the works of his enemies, although one of the Nag Hammadi texts, known as the *Gospel of Truth*, is believed by many scholars to have been written by him. His pre-eminence and wide influence is, however, attested by the Church Fathers, whose most vehement and sustained invective is levelled at 'them of Valentinus', whom they regarded as heretics and hypocrites because they professed the Christian creed but maintained reservations as to its literalness, and also because they practised unorthodox forms of worship (see above, pp.17–18). Valentinus himself was a Christian. Tertullian wrote that the reason he eventually left Rome was that he was passed over for episcopal office, which is a slur that scholars reject as a typical piece of clerical polemic.

The cardinal sins of the Valentinian Christians were, according to Tertullian, pride and presumption. They met in unauthorised assemblies and repudiated authority on the principle that they were all equal, which they carried to the execrable extreme of taking turns to preach and to administer sacraments. 'How frivolous, how worldly, how merely human it is, without seriousness, without authority, without discipline',[9] Tertullian fulminated. What galled the Church Fathers above all was that Valentinus held that the orthodox Christian teaching was crude and elementary and served only to keep devotees in subjection to the Demiurge, the sham god in whose thrall the bishops and priests of the Church were also snared.

Bishop Irenaeus of Lyon insisted that belief in One God was the conditio sine qua non of the Christian faith, but his attempt to beat the Valentinians at the theological game was unsuccessful because they agreed with him, only maintaining that the One God that was the ultimate source of being was not to be confused with the anthropomorphic images of Him as Lord, Father or Judge. As the Church dignitories exercised these latter roles as the putative terrestrial proxies of their God, they could only construe the Valentinian theology as a wickedly casuistic way of subverting their authority and thereby threatening the ecclesiastical order with anarchy. Indeed such would have been its consequence, even if it were not its intention. If Valentinianism had prevailed, the Church would have been more like George Fox's Society of Quakers, a congregation of equals any one of whom might be moved by the 'inner light' to preach or testify his or her spiritual experience.

The supreme achievement attributed to Valentinus himself was the synthesizing of the gnosis, the drawing together of the several traditions of gnostic thought and forming them into a coherent system which embraced a cosmogony, a cosmology, a theology, and an account of the origin, nature and destiny of the world and of man.

The Valentinian system, however, never became a body of fixed doctrine, but rather a framework upon which individuals of the Valentinian schools might weave their own speculative schemes or work towards the experience of gnosis. Extant texts and treatises attributed to the Valentinian movement are by no means consistent, and may even at times seem contradictory, but to denigrate them for this, as the Church Fathers did, is to miss the essential point of the gnostic approach, which eschews conformity as deadening and enjoins active individual exploration and speculation. As St. Paul wrote, 'the letter kills, but the spirit vitalises': a sound and succinct gnostic statement.

Parenthetically, but not irrelevantly in the present context, it may be pointed out that there are distinct gnostic elements in some of St. Paul's writings. For instance, he relates how he experienced being 'caught up to the third heaven – whether in the body or out of the body I do not know', and there learning 'things that cannot be told, which man may not utter' (*II Corinthians* 12:2-4). He speaks of 'hidden mysteries' and 'secret wisdom' which he can only communicate to 'mature' Christians. One to whom he did communicate this arcane teaching was his disciple Theudas, from whom in turn Valentinus claimed to have learned it.

Consider an example of Valentinian variations on a theme (the musical analogy is apt, as it stresses the free and creative nature of gnostic thought). The creation myth outlined in Chapter One, of how the spiritual realms came into being by emanation from the Godhead, and the defective material/terrestrial realms through the folly and passion of the Aeon Sophia, was an essentially Valentinian formulation and synthesis, and we saw in Chapter Two how the Simonian version differed from it in significant details. However, within Valentinian literature there are also significant variations; there are, for instance, different explanations of the motivation of Sophia in begetting the author of the defective creation. Some attribute it to presumption, others to love of the Father, and others to a desire to imitate Him by conceiving by herself, without a male consort (the latter view correlating with the concept of the primordial Godhead as male and his first act of creation being the projection of his dyadic counterpart). Relations between Sophia and the Demiurge are also variously interpreted; some accounts have it that Sophia first brought forth the defective order of creation and then created the Demiurge as agent for its governance, while others maintain that the flawed creation was the work of the Demiurge himself. Furthermore, some Gnostics portray Sophia withdrawing from the creation and unremittingly grieving over her folly, and others represent her as being drawn down into it and there subjected to all manner of suffering and humiliation, while others postulate the existence of two Sophias, the higher one existing in the Pleroma and ever lamenting the contemplation of the tribulations that her counterpart (or in some versions her daughter) undergoes in the lower world. In several gnostic narratives the counterfeit god arrogantly boasts that he is the One God and there is no one above him, a statement which stirs Sophia to admonish him from on high.

The myth of the divine error and fall and of the process of its redemption and the eventual restoration of the integrity of the Pleroma, dramatically represented by the Sophia myth in all its variations, is the core of Valentinian Gnosticism. One of the texts found at Nag Hammadi, and which scholars attribute to a late Valentinian school (about mid-third century), retains the schematic form of the myth, but radically alters the content, ascribing the cosmic catastrophe of the fracture of the Pleroma to a masculine Aeon, the Logos. This Logos, motivated by 'abundant love' and seeking only to 'give glory to the Father', creates other beings, but when he perceives that these are inferior to the creations of the Father, indeed mere shadows and phantoms of them, 'lacking reason and light', he becomes tormented by self-doubt and himself falls into self-division and ignorance, bringing forth more and more defective creatures, 'little weaklings, hindered by the illnesses by which he too was hindered'.

This defective Logos, trapped in his own creation, is interceded for by his counterpart, the Logos in the Pleroma, who co-opts all the Aeons in an appeal to the Father that 'there be aid from above, . . . since the defective one could not become perfect in any other way'.[10] Thus the Father brings forth 'his beloved Son', the Saviour, and despatches him off to rescue the fallen Logos and redeem the defective creation. The Saviour's appearance divides humanity into three classes, the spiritual, who recognize him at once, the material, who reject him, and the psychic, some of whom gradually come to respond to him, the latter category being by implication ordinary Christians and the former the Valentinian gnostic Christians.

This text, which is known as the *Tripartite Tractate*, is clearly an attempt to expunge non-Christian elements, such as the Sophia myth, from the cosmic drama and to produce a version of it more compatible with orthodox theology, and it has been suggested that it was written in response to criticisms by the Church Fathers.

Although structurally and conceptually it is an indisputable gnostic text, one cannot but feel that the gnostic message has become impoverished by such a radical revision, particularly in its exclusion of feminine imagery (except in that the fallen, defective Logos, is characterised as feminine) and in a certain ambiguity about the process of salvation, for while it states the fundamental gnostic principle that salvation is attained through the knowledge that the Saviour brings, it also implies that it can be conferred by the ritual of baptism.

There is no such ambiguity in *The Gospel of Truth*, the Nag Hammadi text which may well have been written by Valentinus himself (the heresiologist Irenaeus attributes a work of this title to him). This reads like a homily addressed to initiates, for the language is often cryptic and allusive, assuming familiarity with the underlying myth of the divine fall and redemption, omitting specific references to the *dramatis personae* and the episodes of the cosmic drama, but continually alluding to it in a manner that initiated Valentinians would understand.

Hans Jonas has proposed that what we have in *The Gospel of Truth* is 'on their own authority what the Valentinians themselves considered as the heart of their doctrine', the 'philosophical core' of Valentinianism, 'stripped of its vast mythological accessories'.[6]

The core is the principle that gnosis alone is the key to salvation, not only in the sense of enlightenment and the elevation of the human individual, but also, and correlatedly, in the universal process of the restoration of the wholeness and oneness of the Pleroma. In other words, the attainment of gnosis by the human individual constitutes a participation in and contribution to the universal process. This is the esoteric meaning of the key passages in *The Gospel of Truth*. For instance:

> Oblivion did not come into existence from the Father, although it did indeed come into existence because of him. But what comes into existence in him is knowledge, which appeared in order that oblivion might vanish and the Father might be known. Since oblivion came into existence because the Father was not known, then if the Father becomes known, oblivion will not exist from that moment on.[10]

The significance of the word 'oblivion' in this context is not clear to the uninitiated, but later in the text the same words are repeated with the substitution of the term 'deficiency', which more clearly refers to the flawed secondary order of creation. This, then, is the core Valentinian doctrine: that the attainment of knowledge by the human individual has positive consequences within the universal order, in fact contributes to restoring that order to its primordial condition of wholeness and unity. *The Gospel of Truth* is a Christian text in that it personifies the bringer of knowledge as the Father's 'beloved son', the Christ, but it does not equivocate the fundamental principle that *gnosis* alone, not any sacrament or ritual, has redemptive power.

MARCION

The teachings of the Gnostic Marcion lack the subtlety and mythic resonance of Valentinian Gnosticism, and indeed lack the conceptual components of gnostic thought that some scholars consider essential, but there can be no disputing the fact that he was profoundly influenced by the gnostic movement and must, if with reservations, be accommodated within it.

Marcion was a wealthy shipowner of the port of Pontus on the Black Sea, and also a bishop. He was in Rome for some time between the years 150 and 160, and apparently was eventually excommunicated from the Roman church for his heretical views. However, his teachings attracted a substantial following and by the end of the second century Marcionite churches had sprung up all over the Greco-Roman world, complete with an ecclesiastical hierarchy, a canon of accepted scripture and forms of worship and ritual similar to those practised in what later became the Catholic Church. There are references to Marcionite churches continuing to exist into the fifth century. Of all the Gnostics, Marcion was the greatest challenge to the institution of the orthodox church, and it has been said that this challenge significantly contributed to the formulation and consolidation of the orthodox creed.

The indisputably gnostic foundation of the Marcionite teaching lies in its postulating the existence of two gods, one the creator and ruler of the known world, the other a 'hidden' and transcendent god, unknown and unknowable in the world because he had no part in its creation. The dualism is absolute, the two gods are in no way related or connected, and although the transcendent god, in his intrinsic goodness, offers human beings liberation from the oppressive power of the god of creation through the intercession of his son, Jesus Christ, this is purely an act of grace, and there is no suggestion that the divine realm is enhanced, or even pleased, when souls find refuge in it from the horrors and pettiness of the lower world.

This uncompromising dualism was inspired less by metaphysical considerations than by the fact that Marcion sought to formulate a Christian faith completely divorced from Judaism and the Old Testament. Yahweh, the God of the Jewish scriptures, was manifestly a spiritually deficient and petty divinity, and attempts to establish concordances between the Old and the New Testaments, by representing events in the latter as having been foretold in the former, and by proclaiming Christ to be the Messiah promised to the Jews, were denounced by Marcion as stratagems for establishing a 'catholic' Church which could accommodate Jewish converts.

Marcion tempered the extreme gnostic view of the Demiurge as incompetent, arrogant and even (in its Iranian versions) fundamentally evil, conceding that the defective god was the god 'of the law' and in his nature 'just', but maintaining that the quality of *goodness* possessed by the God revealed by Jesus Christ was intrinsically different from and superior to the quality of justice. Law and justice are necessary in the lower world to prevent it from disintegrating back into the chaos from which it was formed, but they are unnecessary in and alien to the realm of infinite goodness.

Marcion was thoroughly gnostic in his contempt for the world and for the physical appetites and passions that keep human beings trapped in it and subject to the fickle and oppressive rule of the creator. But there is no 'divine spark' component in his view of the human soul, nor any suggestion that it is exiled from its true home and longs to return there. Human beings are creatures of the lower god, and if they opt to go to the realm of the transcendent God it will not be a home-coming but acceptance of a sanctuary benevolently bestowed. If the good God was sometimes referred to as 'Father' by the Marcionites, the term carried no implications of paternalistic concern for the fate of human souls, but affirmed only God's relationship to his Son, the Saviour. He is God *the* Father, not 'our Father' as in the Lord's Prayer.

Such a view was incompatible with many of the teachings ascribed to Jesus in the gospels. Although in Marcion's day the Church had not definitively settled the question of the New Testament canon, and there existed many gospels other than those of Matthew, Mark, Luke and John, the latter had already been accorded primacy by the Church Fathers. But Marcion accepted none of them as authentic and uncontaminated with interpolations designed to establish the historical continuity and theological concordance of Judaism and Christianity. The Marcionites had a gospel of their own, which they claimed was written by the apostle Paul, but as no copy of it has survived and there is no corroborating evidence that Paul ever wrote a gospel, its content can only be conjectured. The heresiologists said that it was a mutilated version of Luke's gospel – which indeed is the least Judaic and the most Pauline of the four – but the Marcionites specifically denied the allegation. Marcion himself considered Paul to have been the first Christian who had really understood the mission of the Christ, as something to be celebrated as unique in itself and with a significance that Judaistic interpretations only served to obscure, and the scholar G.R.S. Mead suggested that the Marcionite gospel was a collection of the sayings of Jesus used in Pauline churches in his day.

Contempt for the world and its creator led the Marcionites to practise an extremely rigorous asceticism. To take any pleasure in the works of the abominated god of the world, even in food and drink, was to them to betray a weakness that only flattered and consolidated his power, and they sought to limit their use of worldly things to the barest necessities. They abjured sexuality, not on moral principle but because its consequence was to bring more souls into the world and thus aggrandize the realm of the creator. While Christian ascetics were inspired by an idea of the holy life, and believed that their abstentions enhanced their spirituality and sanctity, Marcionite asceticism achieved nothing except a contemptuous rejection of the world and an act of revolt against its creator. In this it was essentially gnostic, and carried into practice a principle that with other gnostics was often no more than a philosophical or literary stance. The Marcionites were not subtle, but they were certainly consistent. Unlike the more sophisticated and intellectual Valentinians, they embraced martyrdom, joyously quitting the world they so utterly despised. This latter fact points to a fundamental difference. The Valentinians rejected martydom because they held that there is no salvation except that attained through gnosis.

The main reservation that scholars have had about classifying Marcionism as a gnostic movement is that the concept of gnosis plays no part in it. Salvation is obtained by faith and conferred by divine grace; this is a position closer to orthodox Christianity than to any gnostic school of thought. The Saviour does not bring esoteric knowledge, nor does instruction or guidance play any part in his mission. His incarnation presents souls with an opportunity they have never had before, to choose between the two gods, to remain in the corrupt fallen world or to accept adoption into the realm of the transcendent God. The Saviour bestows no revelation of the nature of the Father or the soul's afterlife, he simply brings the Good News of their existence and the opportunity to opt for a future state of being utterly different from that which the miserable and benighted soul suffers in the physical world. What miserable and benighted soul could refuse? It is not difficult to understand why the early Church felt more threatened by Marcionism than by any other school of gnostic thought, or why the movement attracted the following that it did.

BASILIDES

When Carl Jung wrote his *Seven Sermons to the Dead*, he attributed their authorship, in true gnostic fashion, to 'Basilides of Alexandria, the city where East and West meet' (see below, pp.111–16). He thus paid tribute to a Christian gnostic philosopher who is believed to have flourished immediately prior to Valentinus, probably about the years 120-130.

Basilides was reputed to have written twenty-four books of commentaries on the gospel teachings, though without specific reference to the versions which later became canonical. He was also said to have written a gospel himself, which he defined as an exposition of 'knowledge of supermundane things', based on the teachings of Matthias (the disciple co-opted to make up the twelve after the suicide of Judas Iscariot), which the latter had received directly from Jesus after the resurrection. Neither this alleged source nor Basilides' own gospel has survived, but it is clear from what can be retrieved of the Basilidian teaching from the writings of its refuters that they would have been esoteric works, expositions of secret traditions intended for initiates and dedicated disciples. Of his own disciples Basilides demanded not only dedication but also a five-year silence, presumably on the grounds that it took that long to take the first steps towards *gnosis*, and even so he declared that only one in a thousand would complete the journey.

When Jung called Alexandria the city where East and West meet this was not only true of the Egyptian city in the second century (there were even Buddhist missionaries there at that

41

time), but it also intimated that the Basilidian teaching syn-
thesised eastern and western spiritual philosophies. Although
the point of departure and the fulcrum of that teaching was the
Christian gospel, Basilides, as G.R.S. Mead said, 'would have
it that the Gospel was also a universal philosophy explana-
tory of the whole world-drama'. When we read the extracts
and summaries handed down in the writings of the Church
Fathers, we are indeed put in mind of the complex speculative
systems of the ancient Buddhist and Hindu metaphysicians,
and also sometimes of the cosmogenic theories of modern
physicists, which it has been pointed out have remarkable
correspondences with eastern philosophies.

Here is Basilides' account of creation and the state of non-
being from which it issued:

> Naught was, neither matter, nor substance, nor void-
> ness of substance, nor simplicity, nor impossibility-of-
> composition, nor inconceptibility, nor imperceptibility,
> neither man, nor angel, nor god; in fine, neither anything
> at all for which man has ever found a name, nor any
> operation which falls within the range either of his per-
> ception or conception. Such, or rather far more removed
> from the power of man's comprehension, was the state
> of non-being, when (if we can speak of 'when' in a state
> beyond time and space) the Deity beyond being, without
> thinking, or feeling, or determining, or choosing, or being
> compelled, or desiring, willed to create universality . . .
> And this universality also was not our dimensional and
> differentiable universe, which subsequently came into
> existence and was separated from the other universes,
> but the Seed of all the universes . . . Thus the Divinity
> beyond being created universality beyond being, positing
> and causing to subsist a single something . . .[8]

In Hindu philosophy the 'Seed of all the universes' is called
Mūlaprakriti, and cosmologists today use the term 'the singu-
larity' to denote the original state of the universe, antecedent
to the 'Big Bang', when all the cosmic material was com-
pressed into a single point; they would have no reservations

in assenting to Basilides' further statement that 'this universal Seed contained everything in itself, potentially'.

Basilides now introduces the concept of 'the Sonship', which he says was inherent in the seed of universal potentiality in three aspects, of different degrees of subtlety.

When the universal seed was sown, the first Sonship separated from it and ascended immediately to unite with the God beyond being. The second Sonship also ascended, though on account of its less subtle nature it needed the help of the wings of the Holy Spirit to do so, but when it arrived at the 'Blessed Space' the Holy Spirit itself could not accompany the Sonship any further, being of a substance and nature incompatible with that space, so it descended again, retaining in itself, however, traces of the second Sonship with which it had been united. In turn these traces permeated everything in the created universe, for everything is suffused with the Holy Spirit.

Now comes the distinctively gnostic aspect of the Basilidian system:

> After this, from the universal Seed and conglomeration of Seed-mixture there burst forth and came into existence the Great Ruler, the head of the sensible universe, a beauty and magnitude and potency that naught can destroy ... Coming into existence, he raised himself aloft, and soared upward, and was borne above in all his entirety as far as the great Firmament. There he remained, because he thought there was none above him ... and thinking himself lord and ruler, and a wise master-builder, he betook himself to the creation of the creatures of the universe.[8]

This, of course, is the familiar Demiurge, but we do not find in Basilides the usual gnostic denigration of his incompetence and arrogance. He is limited, because he is ignorant of the existence of the supercosmic realm of being, but this ignorance is in the nature of things and not reprehensible.

The work of creation which the Great Ruler accomplishes is not of the material world, but of the 'aetherial', otherwise known as the Ogdoad, and in this work he is assisted by his son, whom he has brought into existence from the universal Seed, and who is wiser than his father and therefore 'infused energy into him and suggested to him ideas'. From the father the beings of the aetherial realm receive their bodies or forms, and through the son they become endowed with souls.

Intermediate between the aetherial and the terrestrial realms there is yet another order of being, created and governed by another father-son combination. Known as the Hebdomad, it is the only supramundane world conceived of by men, and its ruler is their God. As to the earth itself, this is the only level where the primordial seed-mixture has consolidated into 'dimensional and differentiable' forms or material substance.

This Basilidian cosmogony, with its several orders of being each inferior to the one above, governed by rulers of correspondingly deficient power and knowledge, is a subtle metaphysical variant of the cosmic drama which in other gnostic traditions was represented mythically and more dramatically. There are no personified deities, no transgressional acts such as Sophia's independent creation, and although each level of being is limited by its ignorance none is reviled for its limitation, nor are there any moral attributions or any imputations of good or evil. Basilides is saying simply that this is the order of things specified by the God beyond being when He deposited the Seed of all the universes.

It is not a static order of things, however. 'All things', says Basilides, 'hasten from below upward, from worse to better'. When the manifold orders of being had emerged from the universal Seed, there still remained within it the third Sonship, which aspired to be united with the other two Sonships and the God beyond being.

There is clearly a correspondence here with the Valentinian concept of the two Sophias, the one in the Pleroma and the other degraded and trapped in the physical world. The Basilidian third Sonship receives its aspiration from the Holy Spirit which imbues it, and manifests in the world as 'the Sons of God', or the 'divine sparks' that have remained in the unrefined seed-mixture in order to 'inform and correct and perfect our souls, which have a natural tendency downwards to remain in this state of existence'.

The aspiration inherent in the third Sonship and in the 'divine sparks' in human beings could accomplish nothing of their own volition. In order that they may be redeemed, the gnosis had to be passed down from the highest level. According to Basilides, this gnosis is the Gospel:

> The Gospel first came through the Sonship through the Son who sits with the Great Ruler; and the Ruler learned that he was not the God above all, but a generable deity, and that above him was set the Treasure of the ineffable and unnameable *That* beyond being, and of the Sonship. And he repented and feared on understanding in what ignorance he had been . . . He began to grow wise through the instruction of the Christ sitting by him, learning what is *That* beyond being, and what the Sonship, what the Holy Spirit, what the apparatus of the universe, what the manner of its restoration.

After the Ogdoad had received the gnosis, it was the turn of the Hebdomad, whose ruler was instructed, again through his son, who received his illumination through the son of the Great Ruler (the Christ). Then:

> The time was ripe for the illumination of the formlessness of our own world, and for the Mystery to be revealed to the Sonship which had been left behind in the formlessness . . . Thus, from the Hebdomad, the Light . . . descended upon Jesus, son of Mary, and he was illumined . . .[8]

As the terrestrial embodiment of the great illumination, the gnosis, Jesus served as the vehicle for communicating it to the third Sonship, which is inherent in human beings in the 'divine spark', and in this capacity he was the Saviour. Salvation is the separation, through purification, of the immortal soul from the mortal and from the physical body. The consummation of the process of salvation will be 'when the whole Sonship shall have ascended, and passed beyond the Great Limit', that is to say into the universality beyond being.

This is not to be construed as a reconstitution of the primordial state of non-being, but rather as the final accomplishment of the original creative act and will of the God beyond being, consisting in everything in the universe existing according to the laws of its own nature. To ensure that this ultimate state of universal order shall no longer be perturbed:

> God will bring upon the whole universe the Great Igno-
> rance, in order that all things may remain in their natural
> condition, and nothing long for anything which is con-
> trary to its nature . . . [For] all things are indestructible
> if they remain in their proper condition, but subject to
> destruction if they desire to overleap and transgress their
> natural limits.[8]

The reader familiar with oriental religions will recognize further correspondences with the Basilidian philosophy. *Tat twam asi* – 'that art That' – announce the Upanishads; *That* being, as with Basilides, the ultimate and ineffable spiritual reality, or deity. The state beyond being to which the soul aspires corresponds with the Buddhist *nirvana*, and the idea of the third Sonship's manifesting in the world as 'the Son of God', whose function is to perfect souls, is like the concept of the Bodhisattvas' relinquishing *nirvana* in order to remain in the world and bring enlightenment to mortal souls.

The Basilidian system also embraced the oriental concepts of reincarnation and *karma*, teaching that the mortal soul may return to terrestrial existence many times, that men may suffer from their deeds in former lives and that it is only the perfected soul, which has received the *gnosis*, or the Gospel, that is immortal.

We do not know whether Basilides was influenced by oriental religions or developed his metaphysical system inde-pendently. In fact, what we do know about this great gnostic philosopher and teacher is only what can be gleaned from a refutational treatise by the Church Father, Hippolytus, which was discovered in 1850 in a monastery library on Mount Athos.

If the original writings of Basilides had not been destroyed the religions of East and West may not have been so different, or at least Christian philosophy would have to be accorded a subtlety and universality equal to the religious philosophies of the East.

A concluding word is called for on the subject of Abraxus (or Abrasax), as the name is frequently met with in gnostic writings, and indeed is prominent in Jung's Basilidian Sermons. The little that was known about the Basilidian school prior to the 1850 discovery included the belief that their god was named Abraxus, and was the ruler of the first out of a total of 365 heavens. As the name Abraxus was found on many talismanic gemstones, the attribution was probably a stratagem for associating Gnosticism with vulgar superstition. Jung's Abraxus, as we shall see, was a deity of awesome magnitude and power, like the Great Ruler of the Ogdoad, but in fact the grounds for associating the name with Basilides are very slight.

CAINITES AND CARPOCRATIANS

The difficulty of extracting truth from a mine of tendentious misrepresentation is ever present when our sole source of information about a gnostic school is the writings of the Church Fathers, and this is particularly so in the case of the so-called Cainites and Carpocratians, for the views ascribed to them were to the orthodox mind perverse and wicked in the extreme.

To esteem the Biblical figures of Cain and Judas, the murderer and the betrayer, does indeed seem morally perverse, but the Cainites had sound gnostic reasons for doing so. Like Marcion, they held the Old Testament god Yahweh to be an inferior deity, and referred to him as the God of generation, as distinct from the superior God of enlightenment and wisdom. Conformity with the laws and commands of the inferior deity was a mark of the unenlightened, whereas rejection and defiance distinguished the enlightened, the Gnostic: hence the honouring of Cain.

The Gospel of Judas was one of the Cainites' basic scriptures.

Neither it nor any summary of its content has survived, but we can recover some of the reasoning behind their reverence for Judas from Irenaeus.

Judas, they held, was a man far advanced in the gnosis. He clearly understood the distinction between the higher and inferior deities, and taught that the spirit that aspires to the higher must completely divorce itself from the works and properties of the lower.

Christ was the spirit descended from the highest plane to triumph over the God of generation and rescue men from his thrall, and he did this by relinquishing his physical (generated) body to death. Judas's 'betrayal' was in fact an act of complicity with Christ's purpose, and he thus contributed to the scheme of salvation.

No known historical figure is associated with the Cainites, but in the case of the gnostic school that the Church Fathers linked with them as being execrably blasphemous in their beliefs and wicked in their conduct, there was a known founder.

Carpocrates was a contemporary of Basilides, and also taught in Alexandria. Irenaeus's account of his teaching was brief and concerned primarily with the doctrine of the transmigration of souls, or reincarnation, which he implied the Carpocratians distorted to provide a rationale for libertinism.

They believed, he wrote, that the soul 'shall not get free from the power of the angels that made the world, but has always to be reincarnated until it has committed every deed there is in the world'.[6] This liberation could, however, be accomplished by some souls in one life. Thus amoral conduct was justified not only because the moral law it transgressed was laid down by the inferior deity, but also because it freed the soul from its prison in nature and the physical by rendering them their due and thereby exhausting their powers. According to Irenaeus: 'At every sinful and infamous deed an angel is present, and he who commits it . . . addresses him by his name and says, "O thou angel, I use thy work! O thou Power of such-and-such, I perform thy deed!"'.[6]

The idea that sinful acts are not only permissible but positively obligatory for the soul that seeks a definitive release from the cycle of birth and death, and that a really dedicated sinner could secure that release in the course of one life, was the extreme of gnostic moral perversity and defiance of the prescriptions of orthodoxy. Irenaeus said that he doubted that the Carpocratians practised what they preached, and Mead maintained that anyway Irenaeus misrepresented them 'owing to his inability to understand the most elementary facts of the doctrine of reincarnation'.[8] Be that as it may, the teaching attributed to Carpocrates was to exert profound and extreme influence in the future, furnishing the philosophy underlying some of the practices of ritual magic and 'Satanism', and influencing literary works from the Faust legend to the transgressive fantasy fictions of the Marquis de Sade.

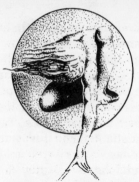

4 · THE GNOSTIC RELIGIONS

With the exception of Marcion, few Christian Gnostics were concerned with institutionalizing their beliefs and practices. Indeed, as we have seen, Gnosticism was in many ways incompatible with ecclesiastical organization, since no organization, save that of the individual of his own spiritual life, could confer *gnosis*. If the concept of salvation through *gnosis* were taken as essential to the gnostic religion, then two movements which developed concurrently with, but largely independently of, Christianity would have to be classified differently. However, historians of religions generally agree that the Mandaean and Manichaean faiths were fundamentally gnostic, and indeed that in its day Manichaeism, which had an ecclesiastical organization that extended westwards to the Atlantic coasts of Europe and eastwards to China, seriously rivalled Catholic Christianity in its bid to establish a universal mass religion.

THE MANDAEAN RELIGION

The Mandaean religion preceded and outlasted Manichaeism, but as it was not a proselytizing faith it remained confined to small communities, and geographically to the valleys of the Tigris and Euphrates rivers in what is now Iraq. Twenty years ago it was estimated that there were still twelve or thirteen thousand members of Mandaean communities in the region. Their name derives from the Aramaic word *manda*, meaning 'knowledge', so 'Mandaean' translates literally as 'Gnostic'. The history of the sect is believed to go back to pre-Christian times, for both Christianity and Judaism are reviled in its literature, where Moses is portrayed as the prophet of the counterfeit god, and John the Baptist is adopted as a true prophet as opposed to Jesus Christ.

Mandaean mythology and theology were based on the Iranian gnostic distinction between the worlds of Light and Darkness, the former governed by a Supreme Being beyond knowledge, and the latter by a King of Darkness, the progeny of Rūhâ, a being descended from but rebelliously opposed to the realm of Light. As in other gnostic systems, the Supreme Being initiated a process of emanation of celestial beings and spheres, each one more degraded than its predecessor, ending with the god Ptahil, creator of the world of man. The King of Darkness participated in this abortive creation, and was also responsible for a creation of his own, of the cosmic spheres and their populations of malign and diabolical creatures. Man was created in his physical being by Ptahil, but his soul had its origin in the realm of Light, where there eternally exists a 'Celestial Adam' whose counterpart, the terrestrial Adam, together with his consort Eve, seeks and awaits liberation from the corporeal and terrestrial prison.

Mandaean scripture, literature and ceremony are primarily concerned with the liberation and salvation of the 'divine spark' through the knowledge conferred by Messengers from the realm of Light. Of the many such Messengers none is ascribed an historical identity, although one was said to have been in Jerusalem at the time of Jesus. But since this Messenger bears the name *Manda d'Haiye*, which means 'knowledge of life', the legend clearly had a polemical rather than an historical foundation.

Mandaean religious ritual focused primarily upon baptism and death, for these were events that concerned the soul.

Mandaean chapels were always located beside running water, which whatever its source was conceived as emanating from the world of Light, so that immersion in it symbolised for the believer a process of cleansing and purifying the soul. Mandaeans would undergo baptism regularly, believing that the ritual maintained the soul's preparedness for its ultimate journey.

The ceremonies that accompanied death were even more elaborate. After the burial of the body – in an unmarked grave because the mortal body was unimportant – ceremonies were held over a period of forty days, the time it would take for the soul to accomplish its journey of ascent to the world of Light if it were not detained en route by the ruling powers of the hazardous intermediate regions that it had to traverse. The dangers of detention were conceived as great, and in addition to ritual help from below in the form of utterance of chants and hymns, the aspirant soul needed to be equipped with knowledge of the nature of the opposing forces it would encounter and the formulae that would appease them.

The Mandaean religion was thoroughly gnostic in this respect, as it was in its mythology and theology, but it became a religion as such, as distinct from a spiritual philosophy, because it did not specify gnosis as the sole condition of salvation, but required that it be prepared for by religious and moral observances by the individual during life and facilitated by the priesthood of the community after his death.

THE MANICHAEAN RELIGION

Mani, the founder of the Manichaean religion, was reared in a religious community which may have been Mandaean, and which certainly laid great emphasis on the ritual of baptism.

Born in the year 216 in Babylon, Mani at the age of four accompanied his father to join the community, where he remained for a period of twenty-one years, although at the age of twelve he underwent a visionary experience in which his vocation as founder of a new religion was revealed to him. At twenty-five a second 'annunciation' led to his breaking away from the community, and accompanied by his father and two disciples he embarked upon a career of preaching the religion that had been revealed to him. Apparently he soon counted members of the Iranian royal family among his followers, and consequently he was allowed to preach and was accorded protection throughout the empire.

Historically, Manichaeism was the most successful and manifest product of Gnosticism. It differed from other gnostic movements in that it did not confine its appeal to a limited number of initiates and did not have any esoteric doctrines. It also differed in that it did not present itself as a version or variant of the Christian teaching.

Mani acknowledged as his precursors Zoroaster, the Buddha, and Jesus, but only in the sense that they too were the recipients of a revelation and mission which, he wrote, 'in this last age . . . arrived through myself, Mani, the apostle of the true God, in the land of Babel'.[6]

He held that the precursor religions had been but partial revelations of the Truth which it was his mission to proclaim in its totality and to all the world.

He himself travelled incessantly, and he organized missionary expeditions by his disciples which established churches in India to the east and in Egypt to the west.

In Iran the royal protection that he enjoyed lasted some thirty years, but in about the year 275 there was a dynastic change and the new ruler, Bahrām I, under the influence of the Zoroastrian priesthood, sought to reinstate the old religion. Mani was arrested, thrown into prison with heavy iron chains fixed to his feet, his arms, and around his neck, and after suffering for twenty-six days he died. His corpse was decapitated and the head exhibited above one of the city gates.

Manichaean missionaries in the Christian world would subsequently refer to Mani's twenty-six days of agony as the 'Passion', and make capital of the ignominious end of the martyred Saviour.

In Iran over the following centuries Manichaeism remained in conflict with traditional religion, suffering periods of persecution but also enjoying periods of prosperity. In the three centuries after Mani's death the religion became a serious rival to Christianity throughout the western world. From a strong base in Egypt, it expanded throughout Asia Minor and North Africa, then throughout the fourth century made steady progress through Dalmatia, Italy, the south of Gaul and into the Iberian peninsula. Saint Augustine was a Manichaean for nine years before he converted to Christianity and became one of its most redoubtable opponents. It was not until the sixth century – and then only by dint of the introduction of draconian laws throughout the Christian world – that the religion was suppressed. But even then its expansion eastwards continued, first throughout central Asia, and then from the seventh to the ninth centuries to China, where successive emperors accorded Manichaeans the right to establish churches and preach their faith. A king of Mongolia became a convert and made Manichaeism the state religion. A Chinese emperor officially acknowledged Mani as the successor of Lao Tzu and the Buddha, and although the religion was persecuted in China in the tenth century it continued to be practised there right through to the fourteenth century.

Despite its worldwide expansion, Manichaeism never had a territorial base where its adherents could be secure from persecution for long. Its rivals, Islam and Christianity, were backed by political and military power, which they employed to expunge the religion of Mani from all the lands they controlled or conquered.

There existed a very substantial body of Manichaean literature in many languages, which included numerous works by Mani himself, but as with other gnostic writings virtually everything was destroyed, and until recent times knowledge of the religion had to be gleaned from the works of its opponents. However, two discoveries in the present century, at Tourfan in Chinese Turkestan in 1900 and at Fayoum in Middle Egypt in 1930, brought to light a body of original Manichaean literature which, though much of it was in fragmentary form, enabled scholars to piece together a clearer picture of what Mani actually taught and how his church was organized.

One of the Fayoum manuscripts, known as the *Kephalaia*, comprises a collection of discourses of Mani with his disciples, and includes passages in which he speaks in the first person. Of particular interest is the account of the visionary experience that he had at the age of twenty-five and which led to his embarking on his mission. On that occasion, he said:

> the living Paraclete came down and spoke to me. He revealed to me the mystery that was hidden from the worlds and the generations: the mystery of the Depth and the Height . . . the mystery of the Light and the Darkness, the mystery of the conflict and the great war which the Darkness stirred up . . . and how the Light overcame the Darkness by their intermingling and how in consequence was set up our world.[6]

The account of his revelation goes on at some length and comprises in condensed form an outline of the Manichaean system.

The system is simple in its conceptual framework, but extremely complex in the mythological elaborations with which Mani embroidered it. It is more uncompromisingly dualistic than the Valentinian and Basilidian teachings, and in this it harks back to an older and less sophisticated gnostic tradition; namely the Iranian, in which deistic dualism was not something engendered in the universe, either by the error or the will of the supreme deity, but was inherent in its very foundations, in the co-existence of two diametrically opposed and irreconcilable principles or natures, characterized by the qualities of Light and Darkness and the corresponding moral properties of good and evil. It was upon this simple and absolute dualistic premiss that Mani elaborated his own version of the gnostic cosmic drama of the divine fall, exile and redemption.

The co-existence of the realms of Light and Darkness was a situation that in no way perturbed the Light, which was content to continue for eternity with the status quo, but the very nature of the realm of Darkness was a constant state of perturbation and internal conflict, and out of this was born a desire to conquer and capture the Light. The ruler of the realm of Darkness, the Evil One, motivated by envy, hate, greed and ambition, declared war upon the realm of Light. This presented a problem for the God of Light, for he had nothing with which to defend his realm, weaponry of all kinds belonging by definition to the realm of Darkness and Evil. So he had to create a Warrior to combat the forces of Darkness, which he did by calling forth the Mother of Life to beget Primal Man.

Primal Man, the first creation, or emanation, of the God of Light, in turn brought forth five Sons, the gods respectively of the light breeze, the wind, the light, the water, and the fire, and with them he 'plunged rapidly from the Paradises downward until he came to the border of the area adjoining the battlefield'. There he encountered 'the Arch-Devil', who, assisted by 'the smoke, the consuming fire, the darkness, the scorching wind, and the fog', overcame Primal Man and his five Sons in battle. The victors devoured the vanquished, and it was thus that the pre-cosmic intermingling of Light and Darkness occurred.

The drama is different from the Valentinian myth, but the gnostic formula corresponds: a part or emanation of the supreme deity falls or descends into the lower world and is there trapped, mixed with a nature that obliterates its knowledge or remembrance of its own nature and origin. Its rescue or redemption is the sequel of the drama. In some Manichaean texts the defeat of Primal Man by the Arch-Devil is more abstractly represented as a victory of Matter over its adversary, Soul, and their consequent mingling, which also requires a further divine intervention to unmix them.

These are pre-cosmic events. The worlds have not yet come into being. God will be compelled to create them in order to establish a mechanism for separating Light from Darkness. But before that the prayer of Primal Man, that he be rescued from the realm of Darkness, must be answered, and to acomplish this a second emanational creation is effected in the sequence:

the Friends of Light, the Great Architect, the Living Spirit. And 'The Primal Man was freed from the hellish substance by the Living Spirit who descended and extended his right hand, and ascending he became a God again. But the Soul he left behind.'[6]

For Manichaeans the liberation of Primal Man was significant as the symbol and guarantee of their own eventual liberation from the Darkness, and it is said that when Manichaeans met they clasped right hands as a sign of their shared belief in salvation – whence originated the greeting common throughout the world today.

Now comes the creation of the cosmos as a closed system, within which the powers of Darkness are confined, and which is the place where the Soul, which has perforce been relinquished to matter, may undergo a process of purification.

Ever bold and dramatic in its imagery, Mani's myth represents the Earth and the boundaries of the Firmament as being made of the carcases and skins of defeated Archons, and the Sun and Moon as consolidations of Light already extracted from the Darkness. These celestial bodies in their revolutions serve as vehicles for transporting Light upward as it is progressively separated out from Darkness.

To undertake this work of separation, God, urged by the Mother of Life, the Primal Man and the Living Spirit, brings forth another god, known as the Messenger. The first stratagem that the Messenger employs is to become manifest in seductive male and female forms to the Archons, who in this system are of both genders, with the result that they 'became agitated with lust . . . and in their concupiscence they began to release the Light of the Five Luminous Gods which they had devoured'.[6] But the Archons simultaneously release a dark substance (sin), which the Messenger and the Angels of Light have to separate from the liberated Light before they can load it onto the vehicles for transportation above. The rejected Dark impurities are cast down to earth, where they become the substance from which the vegetable world is made. The animal world, similarly, consists of abortions conceived by the Daughters of Darkness in their lust for the Messenger.

Seeing himself progressively losing his precious booty of

Light, the Ruler of Darkness resorts to a counter-stratagem, which ironically has been suggested to him by the Messenger's seductive self-revealing ploy. Gathering all the Light left at his disposal, he contrives to procreate two forms modelled on the divine image. Engendered by the copulations of demons, these two beings, Adam and Eve, embody all the captive Light, which through their reproduction and that of subsequent generations, becomes so widely dispersed that the Messenger's task of recovering it is rendered infinitely more difficult.

This is the Manichaean image of man. Modelled on a divine prototype, he is at the same time a mockery of and an insult to the model, for he was conceived by devils and is of their substance. His procreation is the Arch-Devil's work and design. However, this wretched, degraded, vile creature is the focus of the cosmic drama, the prize over which the Powers of Light and Darkness contend, for Light depends upon him for its restoration and Darkness for its very survival.

Jesus figures in the Manichaean myths as the Messenger's own messenger, the agent for the recovery of Light from its fallen and dispersed state. Upon the creation of Adam and Eve, the 'Luminous Jesus' is despatched to awaken Adam, to prompt him to eat from the Tree of Knowledge so that he might discover his true self and understand the nature of things, and initially Adam responds to Jesus and curses 'the shaper of my body . . . who fettered my soul', but he does not heed Jesus's caution against approaching Eve, or rather he tries to but eventually succumbs to her seductions, in which she has the able assistance of demons. It is thus that the reproductive process is set in motion, and that the mission of Jesus is obliged to extend to the human race as a whole and throughout history, until every soul shall be saved and Darkness subdued.

The Manichaean Jesus is not to be identified with the Christian Jesus of Nazareth, nor is there any attribution of specific teaching to him in this system, nor any reference to the exemplary sacrifice and resurrection of the Saviour. One of the things that the Church Fathers found most outrageous about Manichaeism was that it transferred to Jesus the subversive role of the Serpent in the Garden of Eden myth. This was gnostic distortion and provocation at its most infamous. In Mani's system the mission of the Luminous Jesus was to Adam, and the ongoing salvationist work of 'Jesus' will be carried out by other incarnate recipients of the divine revelation and mission, the latest (at that time) being Mani himself.

Jesus as an abstract rather than an historical figure, a symbolic representation of the compromised situation and active function of the divine in its terrestrial existence, is further emphasised by the Manichaean concept of the *Jesus patabilis*, the 'passible Jesus', who is dispersed throughout all terrestrial creation, particularly in the vegetal and animal worlds. One of the things that Jesus shows to Adam is 'his own Self cast into all things, to the teeth of panthers and elephants, devoured by them that devour, consumed by them that consume, eaten by the dogs, mingled and bound in all that is, imprisoned in the stench of darkness'.

The language in such passages expresses an extreme repugnance towards the physical world, both in its nature and its functions. But there is ambiguity here, which arises from the fact that all things are of mixed nature, the Light and the Dark, Soul and Matter, being intermingled in them. This has implications for human conduct, which must be governed by the principle of protecting and cherishing the Light-substance in things while seeking to diminish and stifle the Dark-substance; a principle which enjoins an extreme asceticism and abstinence, particularly with regard to sex and the begetting of children. Mani even prescribes caution when one walks, in a manner reminiscent of Buddhist teaching, lest damage should be done to the Light-substance in plants.

Like all practical religions, Manichaeism did not demand rigorous compliance with its moral prescriptions of all its devotees. It had its ascetic and monastic minority, but the mass of its followers, like Catholic Christians, were regularly absolved from their inevitable transgressions and short-comings in a ritual of confession.

The following passage from one of their manuals of confession conveys at once the similarity and the strangeness of the religion compared with Christianity:

My Lord! We are full of defects and sins, we are deep in guilt: because of the insatiable shameless demon of greed we always and incessantly, in thought, word and deed, and in seeking with our eyes, in hearing with our ears, in speaking with our mouths, in grasping with our hands, and in walking with our feet, torment the Light of the Five Gods.[6]

Where Manichaeism differed fundamentally from Christianity was in its emphasis upon the supracosmic purpose of the work of salvation. Although the believer was urged to live a life conducive to liberating the Light, or soul, within him, this was not stated in terms of 'save your soul'. In its eschatology, or doctrine of the Last Things, there is no Day of Judgement for the individual soul, nor any resurrection of the body. It foresees an ongoing process throughout history of the gradual freeing of the Light, a process which all the mechanisms of the cosmos are designed to facilitate.

The moon is a 'ship of death', conveying souls to the sun, where the divine Light is refined from them and then tansported onward by the wheel of the Zodiac to the supracosmic World of Light.

Ultimately there will remain in the world a small residue of Light so strongly consolidated with Dark that it will require an apocalypse, a great conflagration from beyond the cosmos, to liberate it. In the middle of this raging fire will stand the Hunter of Light, known as the 'Great Thought', gathering into himself all the Light that is released and forming it into the Last Statue, which when perfected will be lifted out of the cosmos by the Living Spirit, who will also form a statue out of the residues of Darkness, which 'he will shut up in the dwelling that was established for it, that it might be bound for ever'.[6]

The visionary sweep and coherence of the Manichaean cosmic drama is impressive, and had the religion prevailed artists would not have lacked inspiration for images every bit as sublime, grandiose and moving as those of Raphael and Michelangelo. That it did not prevail may be partly put down to the repressive efficiency and ruthlessness of the Church

Militant, but other reasons also suggest themselves. Although Manichaeism decked itself out with all the accoutrements of a world religion, with churches, monks, priests, a liturgy, sacraments, scriptures, psalms and hymns, its underlying vision was perhaps too other-worldly, too sublime, too nihilistic with regard to the physical and human dimensions, generally too uncompromising and demanding – in a word too gnostic – to furnish the foundation for a faith of universal and lasting appeal.

5 · GNOSTIC LITERATURE

A strong case could be made for the argument that Western literature owes more to Gnosticism than to orthodox Christianity. Its basic argument would be that orthodoxy, by insisting on the literalness and historical accuracy of its central drama, fettered the imagination to tasks of exposition and interpretation, whereas Gnosticism, having at its heart a drama that is at once cosmic and psychological and that correlates the two, liberated the imagination for work of exploration, speculation and individual expression. Symbolism, allegory, the encoding of meaning in narrative forms or in metaphors, ambiguity and the use of language equally for concealment and for revelation – these are sophisticated literary devices, and gnostic writers have always delighted in them.

Of course, we find myth and allegory in earlier literature, in particular in that of classical Greece. The Greek myths, however, comprised a corpus of historical and religious tradition which was essentially conservative and public and was not open to interpretations of a dissonant or speculative nature. Furthermore, as Julian Jaynes has pointed out, the Homeric heroes lacked subjective consciousness, and the capacity of the human mind to reflect upon itself, its nature, destiny and existential situation, was a later development. It was a development which was supremely exemplified in gnostic literature, which could plausibly claim to be the first substantial body of literature to explore the inner world.

The gnostic ideas of man being in the world but not of the world, and of a bungled and flawed creation in which man is subjected to a kind of cosmic tyranny, were utterly original, and once they had arisen in human consciousness – and in Western literature – they became an intrinsic part of it. Other concepts and narrative themes can be identified that were engendered by the gnostic world-view and developed in its literature, and which have had enduring resonance in literary representations of the human condition: alienation, forlornness, homesickness, spiritual inertia and entrapment, forgetfulness, the fall or descent into a nether world, wandering in darkness, the yearning of the soul, the inner journey or quest, the perils of the quest, the contest with malevolent powers, the seductive lure of the physical and sexual and the revolt against it, the awakening and ascent of the soul, knowledge as the key to liberation.

THE HYMN OF THE PEARL

To illustrate typical gnostic literary devices and themes in a specific context a verse narrative variously known as the *Hymn of the Pearl* or the *Hymn of the Robe of Glory* serves as an excellent example. It is believed that the poem is the work of Bardesanes (c.155-233), one of the original acknowledged great Masters of the gnosis. The poem, which is a first-person narrative, is too long to quote in full, but the following summary incorporates some of the original text in translation.[6]

The narrator begins by telling how, when he was a child, 'and dwelling in my kingdom, in my Father's house' in the East, his parents sent him on a mission to Egypt. Before embarking on the journey, he was furnished from 'the wealth of our treasury' with a large but light load to carry with him. Also he had to relinquish 'the robe of glory, which in their love they had wrought for me' and the purple toga which had been woven and fitted exactly to his figure.

The mission with which his parents charged him was to go down into Egypt and bring back 'the one pearl' which was in the middle of the sea and encircled by a snorting serpent.

63

When he returned with the pearl he would again put on his robe of glory and his toga and together with his brother would be heir in the kingdom.

He set off, accompanied by two royal envoys, who left him when they reached Egypt. He went directly to where the serpent was and settled down nearby in an inn, waiting until the serpent should sleep and he could take the pearl from him. He kept to himself in the inn, and to ensure his incognito he put on clothes like the natives wore. But the Egyptians recognized him as a stranger and treacherously gave him food and drink which put him to sleep, so that he forgot who he was and the mission upon which he was embarked, and thenceforth he served the Egyptians' king.

Aware of what had befallen him his parents and 'all the nobles of the East' sent a letter urging him to awaken, realise who he was and to what servitude he had been reduced, to remember the pearl for which he had been sent to Egypt and the robe of glory and the toga fashioned to his shape which awaited him in his homeland.

Awakened by the bearer of the letter, an eagle, he joyously received its message and his 'free soul longed for its natural state'. He returned to the serpent and charmed it to sleep with an incantation of the names of his Father and of his Mother, then seized the pearl, and after stripping off 'their filthy and unclean garb', left Egypt and set off to return 'to the light of our home, the East'. He was met on the way by royal envoys, who had been entrusted to bring him his robe of glory and his toga.

Having left his Father's house as a child he had forgotten the splendour of the robe, which now he perceived as a mirror-image of himself: 'myself entire I saw in it, and it entire I saw in myself'. Depicted all over it was 'the image of the King of kings' and it quivered with 'the movements of the gnosis'. It spoke as it was borne down to him, saying that it had grown correspondingly with his labours in the world and urging him to clothe himself with it. Thus adorned he returns to pay homage to his Father, to bring him the gift of the pearl and to take his place beside him in his kingdom.

There is a wealth of gnostic symbolism and allegorical

meaning in this simple tale, some of which is obvious and some esoteric. The familiar framework of the quintessential gnostic myth stands out clearly: there exist two worlds, one of light and glory where the King of kings rules, and one of darkness and corruption governed by malevolent powers. The lower world holds captive an element that properly belongs to the higher world and which must be redeemed. The task is assigned to the Son, who descends into the alien world to contend with its ruling powers, initially succumbing to them but ultimately accomplishing his task and returning to the transmundane region, his home.

This is the gnostic significance of the allegorical narrative, and we may note in passing that, typically, it has distinct correspondences with a Biblical story (that of the Prodigal Son), but conveys a different and more profound meaning. Within this basic narrative structure there are individual symbolic components which yield their full meaning only to the reader instructed in gnostic thought and allusion.

Take the 'garment' symbolism. The 'robe of glory' is the heavenly vestment, the garment that the Son has to relinquish so that he may appear in the world stripped of the glory that is his nature but that would compromise his mission if it were revealed. He dissembles by adopting the Egyptians' own garb, but this stratagem also compromises his mission, for dressed like them he becomes like them, unaware and servile. In its esoteric meaning, the 'filthy and unclean garb' is the physical body, which the Saviour must inhabit in his terrestrial existence, while the 'robe of glory' is his spiritual body, to which he returns. When he returns he finds his robe more splendid than he remembers it, for it has acquired virtues corresponding with his achievement in the world, and in fact incorporates in its texture the ultimate achievement, the gnosis. When he puts it on he is united with his perfected self and now appropriately dressed to take his place beside his Father.

The symbolic meanings are multi-levelled and cross—corresponding, so that the key to one may open the secret of another. The pearl is, esoterically, the soul, which it is the Saviour's mission to redeem, but the symbolism of the robe of glory indicates that the work of redemption correlates with the achievement of the gnosis, so the inference is that the pearl, esoterically, represents the gnosis. This interpretation is supported by the ending of the poem. Despite the sacrifices he has made and the perils he has confronted to retrieve the pearl, its recovery is not celebrated, and when it is mentioned it has become 'my Pearl'. What is celebrated is the fact that the Son has fulfilled his Father's orders, and that the Father in turn keeps his promise to elevate him beside Himself. The gnosis is regarded as an objective thing while it is being sought or conquered, but with the success of the mission it merges with the seeker's self.

The journey which the Prince embarks upon is said to be from the East, and at the same time 'downwards' into Egypt. The East is the land of Light, and Egypt the land of Darkness. Some commentators have seen Manichaean doctrine underlying the poem, with the Prince corresponding with Primal Man. Egypt, being the land of the cult of the dead was often associated with darkness, and regarded with abhorrence for the repugnant things that might lurk within it. In gnostic literature it often functions as a symbol for the material world, governed by ignorance and corruption, and by extension for the physical body. The sea, in which the pearl is sunk, is a correlated symbol, likewise representing 'this world', and the 'snorting serpent' or dragon that encircles it stands for the powers of this world. The poem makes much of the Prince's (or Saviour's) essential difference from the world; he is the stranger, the alien, the exile yearning for his home; the clothes he has to wear and the food he has to eat are abhorrent to him, and when he partakes of them he becomes lost, unconscious, enslaved. His situation corresponds with that of the pearl. The Saviour himself has to be saved, the rescuer rescued by a call from the celestial region brought down by an eagle (the Living Spirit of the Manichaean myth, the Holy Ghost of the Christian). He achieves his escape and the rescue of the pearl by inducing in the enemy the condition of sleep and unawareness that they had subjected him to, employing a spiritual power as distinct from their material one.

The material world itself is not redeemed. Its filth and foulness are cast off, left behind, and the transcendent self ascends to be united with its double, or mirror-image, which has awaited his return to the transmundane realm.

THE STORY OF JUDAS THOMAS

This gnostic allegory is contained in a composition entitled *The Acts of Thomas*, and therein it goes under the subtitle *Song of the Apostle Judas Thomas in the Land of the Indians*. This fictitious attribution was characteristic of gnostic literature, where we find, alongside the non-canonical gospels which tend to focus upon the esoteric teachings of the risen Christ and are generally intended for the perusal of initiates, a more accessible religious—romance literature which purports to recount the doings and sayings of the apostles and disciples and to complement the narratives of the canonical *Acts*. The popularity of these works in the second century was such that the Church engaged editors to work over them and try to expunge the gnostic 'poison' and replace it with doctrinally correct material. The *Hymn of the Robe of Glory* may have escaped such revision because of its apparent simplicity and naive charm and because the non-gnostic reader would not construe it as subversive of orthodox doctrine. With regard to the story of Judas Thomas himself, contained in the same text, we cannot be sure that it was not revised, particularly in its conclusion (see p.68).

Judas Thomas, said to be the twin brother of Jesus, drew India by lot as the sphere of his apostolic mission. Arriving there, he was brought before the king, who questioned him about his skills, and upon learning that he was a skilled mason and carpenter commissioned him to build him a palace and furnished him with abundant funds to do so.

The king went away, and Thomas, instead of fulfilling his commission, spent his time preaching the Gospel and spent all the king's money on the poor. When the king sent to ask how the work was progressing, Thomas replied that it was finished except for the roof, for which he needed more money. This was provided and likewise spent. When the king returned and learned from others what Thomas had been doing, he had the apostle flung into prison (where he allegedly wrote his *Song*). Then the king's brother died, and when he saw the heavenly palace that belonged to the king he begged to return to the world to negotiate to buy it from him. Back in the world, he told the king about the palace, describing it so rapturously that his brother refused to sell it, but instead commissioned Thomas to build another one. The two brothers 'received instruction and were baptized'.

There is nothing specifically gnostic about this tale. Perhaps it was laundered by a Catholic editor or written into the *Acts of Thomas* as a red herring, so that the *Hymn of the Robe of Glory* embedded in it might be perceived as equally naive and inoffensive. The latter stratagem would be characteristic of the deviousness that the Gnostics, like the writers of proscribed literature in other times and places, had to practise in order to convey and preserve their message.

THE ACTS OF JOHN

Illegal copying and circulation of texts – *samizdat*, as dissident Russians recently called it – was widely practised in gnostic communities, and it is to the devotion and diligence of copyists that we owe much of our knowledge of Gnosticism. One text was so widely copied that in the eighth century the second Nicene Council had to issue a specific prohibition against doing so, adding that existing copies should be burnt. This was the apocryphal *Acts of John*. It cannot be ascertained when the original was written, but copies existed in the middle of the first century. The putative author is the disciple John, and the main interest of the text lies in the fact that it relates, ostensibly from experience, a mystical account of Jesus's life and teaching.

Like the God-men of Indian traditions, the Jesus of these *Acts* is a being of anomalous and changing physical appearance. When the brothers James and John first saw him, on the shore of Galilee, James saw him as a child beckoning to them, whereas John saw him as a man, 'fair and handsome and of cheerful appearance'. Later John saw him as having a rather bald head but a thick and flowing beard, while James described him as 'a youth whose beard has newly come'. These differences in their perceptions greatly puzzled the disciples, and for John awe was added to puzzlement when he noticed that Jesus's eyes never closed, and that when he prayed he grew immensely in stature and emanated a radiant light.

Such stories can of course be dismissed as exaggeration or hallucination, as can corresponding accounts in Hindu and Buddhist texts, but on the other hand the correspondences could be construed as mutually corroborative and signifying the authenticity of an occult phenomenon manifested only by the most exalted beings.

Another interesting observation of John's, particularly from the gnostic point of view, was that Jesus sometimes held converse with a double, who *descended* to join him. Once when he went to pray on the top of a mountain, the disciples below distinctly heard two voices in conversation. On another occasion, John relates,

> ... when all of us His disciples were sleeping in one house at Gennesaret, I alone, having wrapped myself up, watched from under my garment what He did; and first I heard him say, 'John, go thou to sleep', and thereupon I feigned to be asleep; and I saw another like unto Him come down, whom I also heard saying to my Lord, 'Jesus, do they whom thou hast chosen still not believe in thee?' And my Lord said, 'Thou sayest well, for they are men'.[8]

This could be interpreted as a dialogue between the Christ and Jesus, the heavenly being, the Son, and his terrestrial counterpart or envoy. This distinction in itself, though a gnostic one, was not gravely offensive to orthodoxy, but suggestions that there might be any doubt regarding the terrestrial Jesus's being an unambiguously physical, flesh and blood man, were abominably heretical. In an earlier quotation from the *Acts of John* we noted that, at the very time of the crucifixion, Jesus appeared to and instructed John in a cave on the Mount of Olives. His indifference and insensitivity to the fate of his physical body is stated more emphatically later in the text:

> You will hear that I suffered, yet I suffered not; that I suffered not, yet did I suffer; that I was pierced, yet I was not smitten; that I was hanged, yet I was not hanged; that blood flowed from me, yet it flowed not. In a word, those things that they say of me, I had not, and the things they say not, those I suffered. Now what they are I will shadow forth for you, for I know that you will understand.[8]

One may well ask what all this means. John will understand because he is an advanced initiate in the *gnosis*. Jesus explains to him the mystery of the cross and of his, the Saviour's, real suffering, which he will perforce endure until his mission is accomplished. The explanation bears quotation at length, for it condenses the subtle gnostic Christian message.

> Now the multitude that is about the cross is the lower nature, and those whom you see on the cross, if they have not one form, it is because not yet has every Limb of Him who came down been gathered together. But when the upper nature shall be taken up, and the race which is repairing to me, in obedience to my voice; then that which as yet hears me not, shall become as you are, and shall no longer be what it is now, but above them of the world even as I am now. For so long as you do not call yourself mine, I am not what I am. But if hearing you hearken to me, then you shall be as I am, and I shall be what I was, when I have you as I am with myself. For from this you are. Pay no attention, then, to the many, and them outside the mystery think little of; for know that I am wholly with the Father and the Father with me.[8]

This is the quintessence of gnostic teaching, characteristically conveyed through metaphor and allusion. The Christ manifests in different forms because he cannot be whole until he has liberated and gathered together the Christ-nature (divine spark) in human beings (the metaphor of the gathering of the

Limbs recalls the Osiris myth and illustrates the Egyptian connections of Gnosticism).

The work of redemption is a separating of the lower nature from the higher nature, resulting in the soul's complete transformation and its transcendence of the world. The Saviour's mission is not divine altruism towards the human race, it is work necessary to the reconstitution of the divine universal order. All suffering results from the fragmentation of that order, which is mirrored in the Saviour's situation ('I am not what I am'). It is he, the Saviour, who most ardently longs for salvation and reconstitution, and who most agonisingly suffers (symbolically on the cross, the structure of which delimits the upper and the lower), pending the time of his liberation through humanity's awakening to the gnosis ('then you shall be as I am, and I shall be what I was').

Who shall say that this is not a Christian message, as moving, inspiring and conducive to the religious life as the orthodox teaching? Some might consider that the gnostic view of the Saviour's suffering and need, and of man's implication in it and ability to mitigate, it is less crude and more inspiring (or inspiriting) than the othodox emphasis on the divine sacrifice for the remission of human sin, and the confusedly mixed feelings of guilt and gratitude that it engenders. One can perhaps understand why the *Acts of John* was such a cherished book right down until the eighth century and the dawning of the Dark Ages.

Among other gnostic gems in the *Acts of John*, indeed the one for which it is most celebrated, is an account of a mystic ritual through which Jesus sought to instruct and consolidate his followers on the eve of the crucifixion. He had the disciples form a circle, holding hands, and dance around him. Standing in the centre, he sang a sequence of mystical phrases, to which the disciples had to respond in chorus, 'Amen'. Thus:

The Ogdoad plays to our dancing. – Amen.
The Dodecad dances above us. – Amen.
He who does not dance does not know what is
    being done. – Amen.
To the Universe belongs the dancer. – Amen.

I am a lamp to you who behold me. – Amen.
I am a mirror to you who perceive me. – Amen.
I am a door to you who knock at me. – Amen.
I am a way to you, a wayfarer. – Amen.
Now respond to my dancing.
See yourself in Me who am speaking . . .
Observe what I do, for yours is the passion of
Man that I am to suffer . . .
Who am I? That you will know when I depart.
What I now seem to be, that I am not; but what I
   am you will see when you come.
If you knew how to suffer, you would have the
   power not to suffer
Know then suffering.
That which you do not know, I myself will teach you . . .
In Me, know the Word of wisdom.

The sacred dance never figures in orthodox Christian ritual as
it did in other religions such as the Greek and the Hindu. To the
Church Fathers this portrayal of the dancing Jesus would have
been shockingly sacrilegious, for they regarded such rituals as
the very stuff of benighted paganism. The *Acts of John* may
have been a compilation of scurrilous anecdote and perverse
doctrine conceived to ridicule Jesus Christ and subvert His
Church, as they maintained; but it seems highly improbable
that a literary work so mystical, so philosophically profound
and so imbued with religious feeling and truth should have
been inspired by a merely propagandist purpose.

THE ASKEW CODEX

The *Acts of Thomas* and *Acts of John* were among the few
early gnostic texts known prior to the Nag Hammadi discovery.
Others were contained in what is called the Askew Codex,
which was acquired by the British Museum from the heirs
of a Dr Askew in the 1780s. These manuscripts originated in
Upper Egypt and are Coptic translations from Greek originals
believed, on textual evidence, to have been written quite early
in the second century. They are gnostic Christian works of

considerable length and complexity. Although their contents cannot be briefly summarised, an account of at least the gist of them cannot be omitted from any survey of gnostic literature.

The main text in the Askew Codex is known as the *Pistis Sophia* ('Faith-Wisdom'). It is in the familiar gnostic form of alleged post-resurrection instruction imparted by the spiritual Jesus to the disciples, though it differs from other texts in the same genre by beginning in the twelfth year of such instruction. After eleven years the disciples believed that they had 'received all the fullness', but in fact they had only mounted the first rungs of the ladder of *gnosis*. When they assemble in the twelfth year, on the Mount of Olives, their initiation into the next level is preceded by their witnessing a mystic transfiguration and ascent. Jesus becomes suffused in a radiant light-stream and soars aloft, not to return for thirty hours. When he does return, he 'withdraws his great light into himself, and appears in his familiar form', and proceeds to give them an account of his heaven-journey.

Its purpose was his investiture, his being clothed in the realm of Light beyond the last limit of the firmament, in his robes of glory, three in number, of different degrees of radiance and correspondingly interwoven with different degrees of the gnosis, of knowledge and command of the mysteries. These 'mysteries' relate to the various spaces or spheres of the universe, and comprise the names and the secrets of the powers that govern those spaces. Jesus's passage through the spheres, clad in the appropriate robe of glory, brings to their ruling powers revelation of the existence of the First Mystery (the God beyond being), and results in their conversion. Significantly, each stage of the journey is described as a passage 'upward and inward', which conveys the fundamental gnostic principle that the cosmic order (and disorder) mirrors the state of the human soul.

Arriving in the 'Space of the Twelve Aeons', the Master encounters opposition from 'those of them called the Tyrants', who, 'under their great leader, Adamas, in ignorance fought against the light'. Contending with them, he takes from them a third of their power, 'so that if men should invoke them for evil in their magic practices . . . they should not be able to work their will as before'. Seeing what has happened to the Tyrants, all the other powers of the Aeonic spaces 'adored and sang hymns to the interior of the interiors'.

At the boundary between the twelfth and thirteenth Aeon, the Master finds Pistis Sophia, mourning and grieving because she is excluded from 'her proper region in the height'. The narrative now digresses into an account of the sufferings of Pistis Sophia.

In the beginning she was in the thirteenth Aeon with her companion Aeons. But she looked upwards towards the Light of the First Mystery and, 'longing to ascend into that glorious realm', devoted herself to its worship and ceased to do the mystery of the thirteenth Aeon. Her presumption aroused the hatred of the Aeon, Arrogant, who aspired to rule the thirteenth Aeon, and who joined forces with the twelve Aeons below to bring about her downfall. This they accomplished by projecting their own light, augmented by reflections of the Light above, down into the lower spaces, so that Sophia, mistaking it for the real Light to which she aspired, should be drawn by it downwards towards the regions of Chaos. Her enemies pursued her as she fell, progressively robbing her of her light until it was so diminished that she was trapped in Chaos, the world of matter. Here she grieved unremittingly, but retaining her faith (Pistis) in the Light of lights, she began to sing hymns of repentance.

A long section of the text is devoted to Pistis Sophia's penitential songs. Her devotion initiates the reversal of her situation. She pleads her case that her transgression – quitting her own region – was committed in ignorance and inspired only by love of the Light.

After her seventh repentance the Light forgives her transgression and the process of her liberation from Chaos begins. It is a gradual progression, sustained by her continuing penitential devotions, through which the lower nature into which she has fallen, the nature governed by the powers of matter and desire, is purified, and her own spiritual light-powers are recovered and consolidated.

After the thirteenth repentance her progress is assisted by the light-power of Jesus, which he emanates to clothe her in a new vesture of light in which she might rise higher, but as she rises she is opposed by ever stronger cosmic powers, 'cruel, crafty powers, passions incarnate', which seek to hinder and block her progress. Eventually, with support from above, from the angels Michael and Gabriel, she accomplishes her complete liberation from the bonds of Chaos.

Continuing her upward/inward journey, she comes to the boundary of the thirteenth Aeon, where Jesus finds her, and

> when she saw the radiant light-vesture of the Master, containing the whole of her mystery, the mystery of the thirteenth Aeon, she began to sing a song to the Light which is in the height ... and as she sang, the veils of the thirteenth Aeon were drawn apart.[8]

Concluding the story of the *Pistis Sophia*, Jesus answers questions put to him by the disciples. He then describes to them the glorious beings and spaces that they will encounter as they progress in the gnosis, giving them a foretaste of the spiritual stages that his further instruction will take them through. The disciples are awestruck and daunted by his descriptions, and express their incredulity that mere human beings like themselves should ever be able to reach such lofty heights; whereupon Jesus reproaches them:

> How long shall I bear with you, how long shall I suffer you? Do you not know and understand that you are all ... purgations of the Treasure ... You have been in great afflictions and tribulations in your pourings into different bodies in this world. And after all these afflictions which come from yourselves, you have struggled and fought, renouncing the whole world and all the matter that is in it ... I tell you, the race of human kind is matter. I have torn myself asunder, I have brought them the mysteries of Light, to purify them.[8]

The latter part of the *Pistis Sophia* is devoted to Jesus's instruction as to the nature of the teaching that the disciples should convey to the world.

There is a particularly long and detailed account of the after-life experiences of the soul of the sinner, and of the cycle of reincarnation that the unpurified soul must endure.

There is a novel turn to the eschatology that the disciples are to teach. Human beings must be made to understand that they should not delay their progress in the gnosis in the belief that they will have time for it in future lives, for there will come a time when 'the number of perfect souls shall be completed', and then the gates of the Kingdom of Light will be shut for ever, and souls that have been dilatory in receiving the mysteries will be excluded and consigned to the Outer Darkness.

The other books in the Askew Codex, titled *Extracts from the Books of the Saviour* and *The Book of the Great Logos*, further develop the gnostic Jesus's teachings regarding the mysteries of the Aeonic regions and his instructions to the disciples as to how they may pass through the regions and appease their ruling powers by knowing the appropriate 'seals, numbers and apologies', and how also they may ultimately gain admission to the Kingdom of Light through the knowledge that he gives them of the secret name of the Great Power and of the content of the hymns that they should sing to Him.

THE HERMETIC WRITINGS

All the literature thus far surveyed has belonged to Christian gnostic schools of thought. There have been scholars who maintained that Gnosticism was nothing but an aberrant form of Christianity, but their argument was more polemical than philosophical or historical, and tended to ignore an entire body of literature known as the *Corpus Hermeticum*, which contained hardly any references to Christian or Jewish traditions. The Hermetic writings were composed in the same period – the second and third centuries – as the major gnostic works, and like them emanated from philosophical schools located in Alexandria. They were written in Greek by unknown authors and derive their title from their attribution to 'Hermes Trismegistos' ('Thrice-Greatest Hermes'), a legendary figure who combined the characteristics of the Greek god

Hermes (the fleet messenger between heaven and earth) and the Egyptian god Thoth (god of writing and magic). The writings consist of treatises and dialogues, and although not all of them have gnostic components there are in many of them distinct correspondences with and variants of fundamental gnostic ideas which support the argument that Gnosticism had a thriving existence quite independent of Christianity.

One of the main treatises in the Hermetic literature is an account of a visionary experience of the writer which vouchsafes him a revelation of cosmic, terrestrial and human origins and destiny. The treatise is titled the *Poimandres* ('Shepherd of Men'), because the Presence that conferred the revelation identified itself by that name, adding that it was also 'the Nous (Mind) of the Absolute Power'.

This attribution points up a basic difference between Christian and Hermetic Gnosticism, in that in the latter there is no intermediary figure between the Godhead and the recipient of the *gnosis* and consequently no saviour-figure to serve as the soul's exemplar, instructor or guide in its aspiration to return to the divine realm. Another notable difference is that the highest God and the creator, or Demiurge, are not designated as opposed or antithetical powers, and consequently the cosmos and the material world are regarded as deficient but not degenerate orders of being and there is no expression of the characteristic gnostic repugnance toward the physical and material.

These are substantial differences, but on balance they do not outweigh the similarities that indicate that Alexandrian Gnosticism in the second century was a highly diversified philosophical movement.

In the *Poimandres*' account of creation there is the familiar Light/Darkness dualism. The revelation begins when Poimandres changes his form and the visionary beholds 'a boundless view, everything become Light, serene and joyful'.[6] But presently 'there was a Darkness borne downward ... appalling and hateful, tortuously coiled, resembling a serpent', which becomes a humid, smoking substance. Into this substance, the Nous, or Light, sends his emanation, the *Logos* (holy Word), which has the effect of separating, through incandescence, the heavier and lighter elements. Thus begins the work of bringing order into the universe. The text is not clear as to why the Darkness came into being in the first place. The familiar gnostic explanations, either that it had always co-existed with and in opposition to the Light, or that the successive emanations from the Godhead were in the nature of a divine fall and progressive loss of control, are not invoked. When the writer asks whence the elements of nature arose, he receives from Poimandres the answer that a female divine principle, the *Boulé* (Will) sought to 'fashion herself into a cosmos according to her own elements and her progeny'. This suggests a parallel with the Valentinian Sophia myth, but when the Demiurge is introduced, as he is at this point, it is not as an emanation of the female principle, but rather as a direct emanation from the Absolute Power.

This Demiurge is the Nous-Artificer, and to accomplish his task of bringing order to the cosmos he appoints seven Governors of seven spheres which encompass the material world. Collectively they constitute *Heimarmene* (Destiny), the governing principle of the cosmos. With the establishment of this order the Logos, the original divine principle that initiated the separation of the elements, withdraws from the physical creation, leaving Nature bereft of reason, and reduced to mere matter.

We come now to the creation of man, the most original and influential aspect of the Hermetic speculation.

Man is the third order of divine creation after the Logos and the Demiurge, but by no means an inferior one. He is created by the Absolute Power in His own image and is so beautiful that 'even God became enamoured of his own form, and delivered over to him all his works'.

Perceiving the order created by his brother, the Demiurge, the divine Man enters into it and travels down through the spheres of the seven Governors. There is no specified reason for this divine descent, nor any suggestion that it was a transgressive act, although it does have tragic consequences. Descending through the cosmic spheres, Man is admired by the Governors and receives from each of them by way of tribute a portion of his nature and powers.

He comes at last to the terrestrial plane, where Nature,

beholding in him the beautiful form of God combined with all the powers of the Governors, falls in love with him.

He reciprocates, 'seeing his likeness present in her, reflected in the water, and, conjoined with her sexually he comes 'to inhabit the form devoid of reason'. This then is the human situation:

> This is why alone of all the animals on earth man is twofold, mortal through his body, immortal through the essential Man. For though he is immortal and has power over all things, he suffers the lot of mortality, being subject to the Heimarmene; though he was above the Harmony, he has become a slave within the Harmony; though he was androgynous, having issued from the androgynous Father, and unsleeping from the unsleeping one, he is conquered by love and sleep.[6]

The first progeny of the union of Man and Nature are seven beings whose natures correspond with those of the seven Governors. Thus these characteristics are bred into the human race. In the account of the divine Man's receiving a portion of the Governors' endowments it appeared that these were gifts of a positive nature, but now it turns out that they were not so, on the contrary they were attributes that compromised the divine nature before it definitively compromised itself by falling into Nature.

As in other gnostic systems the fall is the prelude to an ascent, and it is in the *Poimandres*' description of the ascent of the soul after being liberated from the physical body at death that the Governors and their characteristics are portrayed in their true colours; the ascent is described as a progressive relinquishing to the cosmic powers of appetites, passions and conduct which constitute the soul's impurities and corruption. This is a rendering back to the Governors of the ambiguous gifts that they conferred upon divine Man in the journey of his descent, a liberating of the soul from the degenerate accretions that it acquired through its fall into matter and a process that ultimately enables it to transcend the cosmic Heimarmene and re-unite with the Godhead.

Hermeticism is distinguished from Christian and Manichaean Gnosticism by its diminished emphasis upon – one might even say avoidance of – the subjects of sin and evil. None of the protagonists in the cosmic drama is evilly motivated. The Demiurge is brought into being to make the best of an unfortunate situation, the existence of the primordial Darkness and Chaos, which itself is not put down to any transgression. Divine Man embarks on his cosmic journey prompted by nothing more reprehensible than curiosity, and when he falls in love with Nature it is not a succumbing to the seductive lure of the physical but a narcissistic response to his own image reflected in her. The Governors are only seen as embodiments of negative characteristics by implication, and even so those characteristics are regarded as encumbrances to the soul's ascent rather than as evils. If they behaved malignly and subversively in passing on their characteristics to Man, the text does not draw attention to the fact. In the *Poimandres* and the *Corpus Hermeticum* generally, we do not find the nihilism, pessimism and moral dualism and absolutism characteristic of other gnostic literary works. In fact, with its emphasis on the inalienable divinity of man which may be compromised but cannot be effaced, the Hermetic philosophy constituted a form of optimistic and humanistic Gnosticism, which explained why it resurfaced as a profound influence upon Renaissance thought in Europe more than a millennium after its Alexandrian flowering.

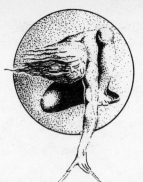

6 · THE LEGACY OF GNOSTICISM

By the sixth century the Roman Catholic Church could account itself triumphant over Gnosticism and the rival Manichaean religion, but although its victory was politically conclusive it was by no means definitive, and right through until the fifteenth century there was scarcely a time when the troops and inquisitors of the Church were not waging war on some heretical sect whose beliefs and religious practices were fundamentally gnostic. A full history of these resurgences would require a separate book, and in the present context only a brief survey of the main ones can be attempted, to show that although most of its literature was destroyed, the essential ideas and beliefs of Gnosticism proved remarkably enduring.

In the early seventh century there arose in Armenia a movement known as Paulicianism, which for over three centuries flourished in the eastern territories of the Byzantine empire and had followers in Constantinople itself. It constituted a formidable threat to the orthodox Byzantine Church, for it not only had an ecclesiastical order and established churches itself, but also had powerful political and military supporters. The tenets of the religion that it promoted included a dualism based upon the opposition of the creator God, the ruler of the present and visible world, to the true God, Lord of the invisible and future world, a rejection of the Old Testament, of the reality of the Incarnation, and of the sacraments, forms of worship and hierarchy of the orthodox Church. It was not until towards the end of the tenth century that Paulicianism succumbed to the superior power of the Empire, whereupon many of its devotees were deported to nearby lands where they continued to practise their faith and to proselytise.

BOGOMILISM

One of the countries they went to was Bulgaria, and their influence was certainly a factor in if not the direct cause of there arising in that country the movement of Bogomilism, so-called after its founder, who was known to his followers as 'the Pope Bogomil'.

Originally a member of the lower clergy of the orthodox Church, Bogomil led a movement that was politically nationalistic and revolted against the imported Byzantine orthodoxy and the higher clergy who supported it, condemning the latter for their luxurious and self-indulgent life-style and advocating a return to the original Christian message which was construed as enjoining the ascetic life, abstinence from all but simple basic foods and from marriage and the procreation of children.

In a letter to the tsar of Bulgaria written in about 940, the Patriarch of Constantinople referred to Bogomilism as 'Manichaeism mixed with Paulicianism'. The Bogomils referred to themselves as 'Friends of God', and they denounced the orthodox Church as the creation of Satan.

Throughout the eleventh and twelfth centuries the Bogomil church expanded beyond its Bulgarian base to the Balkan countries and the coasts of Asia Minor. It extended to Russia in the fourteenth century, and in Bulgaria itself it retained a following right up to the seventeenth century.

A comprehensive picture of what the Bogomils believed and taught can be gleaned from the writings and the ecclesiastical records of their orthodox opponents.

They rejected the authority of the Old Testament, and although they held in high esteem the books of the New Testament they contested the orthodox interpretation of their content and maintained that certain sayings of Jesus had been excised from the Gospels; for instance, 'Honour the demons, not because they are useful to you, but so that they may not do you harm'.[3] They referred to Matthew's account of the temptation of Jesus, and maintained that the high mountain from which Satan showed him all the kingdoms of the world was in fact his domain, the second heaven, and that his offer to give the kingdoms of the world to Jesus clearly implied that Satan was sovereign over them because they were his creation.

Satan was held to be the eldest son of God. In a Bogomil myth of the fall and creation, Satan, resenting his subservience to the Father, conscripted from among the angels those who were similarly rebellious and mounted an abortive uprising against the Father, who forthwith expelled the traitors from heaven. As the son of God, Satan retained all the divine power, and exercised it to create a second heaven where he might reign supreme, further extending his sway by creating the earth and all that it contains. Out of terrestrial matter he modelled the first man, Adam, but when he sought to animate him with his own breath he produced an abortion, the serpent.

Satan appealed for help to the Father, promising Him that man would belong to them jointly and that through his progeny the heavenly seats vacated by the fallen angels would be reoccupied. God in His goodness consented to animate Satan's creation with his breath. Eve was likewise created of divine breath (soul) and satanic substance (body).

Jealous of the divinity that his creatures embodied, and in order to prevent its being passed on to their progeny, Satan contrived with the help of the serpent to inveigle Eve to unite with him, and thus was born Cain. Eve's second son, Abel, was murdered by her satanic offspring.

Satan was punished for his transgression with Eve by being stripped of his divine form and powers, though he was allowed to retain sovereignty over his creation.

As this summary demonstrates, the Bogomils, although they rejected the authority of the Old Testament, adapted some of its mythic narrative to their doctrinal cause. Interpreting the statement in *Genesis* that the sons of God, finding the daughters of men beautiful, united with them and produced a race of giants, they identified the divine progenitors with the fallen angels, and extended the story to tell how the giants proclaimed to mankind the truth about Satan and the cause of his expulsion from heaven, whereupon Satan destroyed both mankind and the giants by means of the flood, sparing only Noah because he had no daughter and had not participated in the revolt but had remained faithful to the lord of creation.

The Bogomils carried the denigration of the origins and nature of man implicit in these myths into practice in their repudiation of procreation and by regarding young children with abhorrence as creatures of Satan, who they held was present in every conception and throughout prenatal and postnatal existence, and who could only be driven from the body in later life by a rigorous regime of asceticism and religious observance. Their aversion to the process of physical procreation led to their denying the literalness of the Gospels' account of the nativity. According to them the virgin Mary found the Christ child in a cave, and although he appeared to have corporeal substance and form this was an illusion. He adopted apparent physical form in order to accomplish his mission and preach the gospel, but his passion, death and resurrection were all a charade. Likewise, the miraculous healings attributed to him were of spiritual rather than physical infirmities, and were in reality remissions of sins.

The Christ's terrestrial mission included the visitation of the ultimate divine punishment upon Satan, whom he despatched into the depths of the earth shackled by a heavy chain.

Having accomplished all that he had come to do, the Christ returned to be united with the Father, leaving mankind to struggle to accomplish salvation through the teachings he had given them. One of the sayings allegedly excised from the Gospels was: 'Save yourself by whatever manner you may'. Their opponents regarded this as a Bogomil invention to exonerate their duplicity in professing compliance with orthodox beliefs when in danger of being persecuted for heresy.

The Bogomils rejected the rites and sacraments of the orthodox Church. They scorned veneration of the cross, arguing that 'if someone killed the king's son with a piece of wood, could the king regard the weapon as holy?'[3] They practised baptism, but not by water, for they regarded John the Baptist as the precursor of the Antichrist. Their rite demanded of the candidate a long period of ascetic preparation and intense prayer, and consisted in a 'minister of the great mystery' placing his hands holding the Gospel on the candidate's head, invoking the Holy Spirit and reciting the *Pater noster*. The baptism was confirmed by repetition after another long period of prayer and abstinence, the strict observance of which had to be confirmed by witnesses. These rigours were considered necessary in order to release the soul from the controlling power of Satan and render it pure, perfect and fit to enter the realm of the Father, when eventually the 'tunic' of flesh was cast off.

Clearly this was not a process that the majority of the congregations of the Bogomil church would have been willing or able to undergo. We know that regular fasting and prayer were required of them, and that there was a practice of confession of sins. They did not observe the Christian festivals and saints' days. It was an austere and demanding religion, and the fact that it flourished so widely and as long as it did testifies not only to the zealous medieval concern for the fate of the soul, but also the failure of a self-indulgent, duplicitous and often rapacious orthodox clergy to command the respect of ordinary people.

CATHARISM

Disrespect for the clergy on account of their worldliness, and resentment at their extorting tithes by threatening or applying the ultimate sanction of excommunication, was certainly a factor that contributed to the appeal of Catharism in Europe in the twelfth and thirteenth centuries.

We know much more about the Cathars than about the Bogomils, for meticulous and detailed records were kept of the inquisitorial proceedings to which they were subjected.

There is a clear line of descent between the two movements. In the eleventh century the Bulgarian heresy was flourishing in Northern Italy, particularly in Lombardy and Tuscany, and we have it on the authority of the Inquisition that in the thirteenth century leading Cathars from the Languedoc in France went to Lombardy to be initiated as *parfaits*. In fact so close were the ties that it is misleading to speak of two movements, and more accurate to conceive of a gnostic resurgence extending from Asia Minor to Spain and northwards to Flanders. In 1167, for instance, a Cathar Council held at St. Félix de Lauregais in the Haut Garonne region of France was presided over by a Bogomil bishop from Constantinople.

Catharism is most closely associated with the Languedoc because it was there that the most appalling and dramatic events of its persecution were enacted and the most detailed historical records were brought to light. However, the name 'Cathar' was of German origin, and first applied to heretics burnt at the stake in Cologne in 1143. In the first half of the twelfth century Catharism was rampant in Germany, Flanders, northern and eastern Spain, and throughout France. Those who participated in the movement did not call themselves Cathar – the term was only used by their denigrators – but 'the Poor of Christ', 'the Friends of God', 'the good Christians', or simply 'the Goodmen'.

There were Cathars at all levels of society, from the highest nobility to the simplest shepherds, and the faith did not lack sympathisers among the clergy themselves. One of the reasons why the Cathars became entrenched in the Languedoc was that for some sixty years before the first bloody 'crusade' against them in 1210 they enjoyed relative security there, because the local ecclesiastical authorities lacked the military backing to police such a large area and to act upon a Papal declaration of 1179 which called for the extermination of the heretics. There were even public debates and disputations held between learned Cathar *parfaits* and doctors of the Church.

The first mass incineration of Languedoc Cathars occurred

at Minerve near Carcassonne in 1210, when 140 were put to the stake. There followed a series of 'crusades' culminating in the fateful last stand in the formidable high castle at Montségur, which fell to a Catholic army in 1244 after a ten-month siege. A total of 225 Cathars were burned that day. The Church was victorious, but the heresy was by no means wiped out. It took nearly another century of diligent 'mopping up' operations by the Inquisition to eradicate it.

An enthralling book by the French historian Emmanuel Le Roy Laduric reveals how tenacious the Cathar faith was. *Montaillou*, its title, is the name of a remote village in the high Ariége, close to the Pyrenees. Catharism was rife here in the early fourteenth century, and from the Inquisition Register of Jacques Fourier, the local bishop who was later to become Pope Benedict XII, Laduric gleaned a comprehensive picture of the life of the humble peasant community of Montaillou, where itinerant *parfaits* converted most of the population to Catharism, including eventually the village priest.

A *parfait* was a person who had undergone the sacrament of baptism by book and word (in the manner instituted by the Bogomils). Thereafter, he (or she – the religion was not sexist, there were also *parfaites*) had to live an ascetic life, abstaining from meat, wine and sex, and was empowered to confer the sacrament of baptism upon others, making them also *parfaits*. However, as the abstentions that the status demanded were not practicable for the majority of people, the sacrament was generally administered when someone was close to death, and was then known as the *consolamentum*. Among the martyrs of Montségur were twenty ordinary believers who became *parfaits* and *parfaites* just before the final capitulation. So, in effect, although most Cathars became *parfaits* there was an elite who were highly respected for their uncommon dedication and asceticism. Most had professions, for instance as weavers or shepherds, but their missionary work required much travel, and to provide them with food and shelter was considered a duty and an honour by ordinary believers.

When a *parfait* was guest in a household, people would congregate to hear what he had to say and to discuss questions of religion with him. It was in such informal circumstances that Catharism was promulgated. Sometimes a *parfait* would be accompanied by followers as he travelled and would preach to them *en route*. Much of the teaching was conveyed in anecdotes and parables, several examples of which are given in *Montaillou*. For instance:

> There is a bird called the pelican: its feathers shine like the sun. And its vocation is to follow the sun. The pelican had some young. It left them in the nest, so as to be able to follow the sun more freely. During its absence, a wild beast got into the nest and tore off the nestlings' claws, wings and beaks. After this had happened several times, the pelican decided to hide its radiance and to hide among its young so as to surprise and kill the beast when it next came into the nest. And this the pelican did. And the little pelicans were delivered. In the same way Christ hid his radiance when he was incarnated within the Virgin Mary; thus was he able to take the bad God prisoner and shut him up in the darkness of Hell. And thus the bad God ceased to destroy the creatures of the good God.[7]

Thus were conveyed to simple peasants the fundamental gnostic ideas of the opposition of the good and evil gods, the identification of the good God with the realm of light, and the Saviour's incarnation as a subterfuge. Similar parables taught the incompatible dualism of body and soul and the possibility of the reincarnation of an unredeemed soul in the body of a lower animal. Myths of the creation and fall were likewise conveyed in simple and dramatic terms.

The reader will recognize distinct gnostic themes in the following extract from an account of a Cathar gathering at a house at Arques, in the Aude region, in 1300:

> The *parfait* Jacques Authié read from a book, and his father, the *parfait* Pierre Authié [one of the most distinguished and learned Cathars, by profession a notary] explained in the vulgar language, saying: 'The souls, after falling from heaven to earth, remembered the good that

they had abandoned and lamented the evil that they had found. The devil, seeing them sad, told them to sing the hymn of the Saviour, as they were wont to do. They replied: "How can we sing the hymn of the Saviour in an alien land?" One of the souls even said to the devil, "Why did you trick and seduce us into following you and leaving heaven? You have gained nothing, for we shall return there". The devil replied that they would not return to heaven, for he had made for them tunics [of flesh] from which they could not escape and in which they would forget the good and the joy that they had had in heaven.'[3]

The myths and parables by means of which the Cathar missionaries conveyed their teachings would be repeated and discussed by people as they went about their work or in their social and family relationships. Many who continued to profess and practise orthodox Catholicism found the teachings of 'the goodmen' appealing and convincing, and particularly with regard to the all–important issue of salvation many trusted and preferred the *consolamentum* administered by a *parfait* to the sacrament of last rites administered by a priest. A typical attitude was expressed by the Montaillou shepherd Pierre Maury:

It's no good confessing to the priests. They keep whores, and all they want to do is eat us up, as the wolf destroys the sheep . . . It is better to be received into Belibaste's [a *parfait*] sect just before death. Then you are absolved of your sins, and in three days, after you are dead, your soul ascends to the Heavenly Father.[7]

Cathars referred to the sacrament of being received into the sect of the *parfaits* as being 'hereticated'. The term would seem to imply that they acknowledged the faith as a heresy, but for them the word did not connote error or deviance as it did when used by the orthodox. They considered that theirs was the true Christianity and it was that of the Church of Rome that was deviant.

The book that every *parfait* always carried for the purpose of baptism was the New Testament, but the Cathars, like the Bogomils, held to unorthodox interpretations of its content and considered some of its component texts more authoritative than others, and that in some cases the 'letter' of the text had been tendentiously altered by the Church. Jacques Authié said in 1305, when he was arrested by the Inquisition:

> There are two 'letters', one of which is ours, and which the Son of God gave us when he came into this world, and this is true, reliable and good; but after the Son of God had given it, Satan created an imitation which is false, evil and unreliable, and it is this that the Church of Rome holds to. If those of the Church of Rome saw the original, few among them would recognize it, for they are blind; and although there may be some among them who would understand it, such is their attachment to the world that they would hide it from others and not wish to follow it.[3]

Cathar *parfaits* were brave men indeed to make such statements before the Inquisition and suffer the inevitable consequences. Eventually the efficiency of the Inquisition tracked them all down, and the ordinary people, deprived of the instruction, the example and the sacraments of 'the good-men', reverted to compliance with orthodoxy. Catharism was completely wiped out by the mid-fourteenth century, but its oppressors could not foresee the Reformation of two centuries later, a movement of greater historical significance of which Catharism was undoubtedly a precursor.

HERMETICISM

We saw in the last chapter that there were affinities between the Hermetic and gnostic traditions, although fundamental differences make it disputable whether Hermeticism can be regarded as a gnostic movement. A vast literature exists on the subject of the Renaissance revival of Hermeticism, which it would be neither possible nor appropriate to attempt to review in the present context, but the connections between the two movements were originally, and remained, significant, and a survey of the gnostic legacy would be incomplete without at least a brief commentary on the revival of the Hermetic tradition.

It began with the acquisition, in 1460, by the ruler of Florence, Cosimo de Medici, of several of the texts of the *Corpus Hermeticum*, including the *Poimandres*, and their translation from Greek into Latin by the court scholar, Marsilio Ficino. The Church was remarkably tolerant of the Florentine intellectuals' enthusiasm for the rediscovery of the lost literature and pagan tradition, and did not regard it as a resurgence of the hated gnostic heresy. Hermes Trismegistos was a respectable figure, for early Christian writers including St. Augustine had written favourably of him, even putting him on a par with Moses. In fact there is a fifteenth century engraved flagstone in the Cathedral of Sienna which represents Hermes and Moses together. There were certainly texts in the *Corpus Hermeticum* that could not have been congenial to the orthodox – writings on astrology, alchemy and magic, for instance – but they appear not to have been regarded as subversive, perhaps because it could be argued in their defence that the 'three wise men' who paid homage to the infant Jesus were magi and astrologers. But the primary reasons for the tolerance of the revival were that the movement did not challenge orthodoxy directly and did not seek a following, and its devotees could be marginalised as a minority of intellectuals and esotericists.

The Renaissance was the emergence from the 'Dark Ages' of ignorance and dogma, the rediscovery of the light of ancient knowledge, and the assertion of man's potentials for spiritual effort and growth. Light, knowledge, spiritual growth: these are basic gnostic concerns, even if in Hermeticism they were associated with a philosophy disposed to affirm life and the world rather than negate them.

Emphasis on the duality of human nature is also common in Renaissance philosophy, but again with a positive implication, namely that man is privileged to be endowed with a portion of divinity and with a capacity to choose whether to develop and exalt it or to ignore and diminish it.

The concept of the Divine Man of the *Poimandres* undoubtedly influenced the philosopher Pico della Mirandola when he composed what amounted to the ideological manifesto of the Renaissance, his *Oration on the Dignity of Man*. In it he imagines God addressing man and telling him that of all the beings in creation he alone has free will:

> You have the power to degenerate into the lower forms of life, which are brutish. You have the power, out of your soul's judgement, to be reborn into the higher forms, which are divine. Whatever seeds each man cultivates will grow to maturity and bear in him their own fruit. If they be vegetative, he will be like a plant. If of the senses, he will become brutish. If rational, he will grow into a heavenly being. If intellectual, he will be an angel and a son of God. And if, happy in the lot of no created thing, he withdraws into the centre of his own unity, his spirit, made one with God, in the solitary darkness of God, who is set above all things, he shall surpass them all.[2]

The dualism of the heavenly and the degenerate orders of creation and of the divine and brutish components of human nature is pure Gnosticism, as are the concept of the soul's destiny to be reunited with the divinity 'set above all things', and of the way to that fulfilment being an inner journey to 'the centre of his own unity', through the intellect and the knowledge it attains.   Later in his *Oration* Pico specified the kinds of knowledge that lead to such fulfilment, giving prominence to the sciences of number and of *Mageia*, or magic. He was careful to distinguish between the magic that involves the invocation of demons and the use of their powers and that which involves an intense contemplation upon and profound comprehension of nature and the divine mind, which confers the power 'not so much to work wonders as to serve a wonder-working nature'.

The question of the relationship of the Hermetic and gnostic

traditions to magic and occultism must be addressed. It went
back a long way. Simon Magus was derided as a mere magician, a wonder-working charlatan. The gnostic cosmogony,
with its hierarchy of cosmic spheres and their governing
powers and its concept of the soul's progress as dependent
upon frustrating or appeasing those powers, comprised in
effect a magical view of the universe. When the Jesus of the
Book of the Great Logos taught his disciples the appropriate
'seals, numbers and apologies' for the various stages of the
cosmic journey, he was in fact giving them instruction in
ritual magic. All magic is about power, and power derives
from knowledge, and it is thus that the attainments of *gnosis*
and *mageia* are closely correlated. The distinction between
the two kinds of magic, black and white, is the distinction
which Pico made between the power that seeks to coerce
and the power that derives from profound understanding.
Fundamental to the gnostic philosophy is the principle that
occult powers exist, and that ignorance of or indifference to
their existence keeps the soul entrapped. Gnostic nihilism,
with its view of nature and the world as totally alien and
hostile to the soul, regarded the occult powers as invariably
sinister, characterised them in its mythology as devils or
demons, acknowledged that man could co-opt their powers
in his worldly projects, but maintained that the fulfilment
of the soul's project required their defeat and submission. It
enjoined an extreme asceticism, for it regarded the sinister
occult powers as intrinsic to human nature as well as having
an objective existence in the cosmos.

Hermeticism, on the other hand, was based on the belief that
the occult powers were not uniformly malevolent, but that
there existed in nature and the world, and in man, powers that
could be co-opted to the purpose of the soul's transcendental
project. The 'magic' that Pico advocated was the science of
working with those powers.

'Science' may appear to be an inapposite term in this
context, for it is commonly believed that the scientific view
of the universe superseded the magical view and that science
demonstrated that belief in magic was mere superstition and
ignorance. But 'science' means 'knowledge', and it was not

the view of the Renaissance Hermeticists that the realm of the knowable is limited to the material world.

Are we to call alchemy magic or a science? The so-called 'royal art' of the Hermetic philosophers can be seen superficially as a pseudoscientific quest for a means of transmuting base metal into gold, but this quest was in fact an analogue of the gnostic striving to liberate the divine element imprisoned in matter, to transmute the alchemist's own spiritual substance by ridding it of contaminating impurities and thus enabling the pure soul or spirit to become manifest and free.

In Hermeticism, more than in any of the known gnostic schools, specific strategies for accomplishing the work of transformation, which is the attainment of *gnosis* and the liberation of the soul, are made explicit. All rest upon the belief that the 'divine spark' in man is not a mere inert and alien residue locked into the material world and longing to transcend it, but is an attribute that retains its endowment of divine power, and can exercise that power to bring about change both in the world and in the self.

Magic and alchemy were two such strategies, and astrology was a third. All lent themselves to debased and superstitious practices, but at their loftiest they brought together imagination, will and knowledge to constitute a powerful spiritual force.

Fundamental to Hermeticism and to the practices and strategies that it developed was the principle that there exist occult connections, relations and influences between seemingly disparate things. To Hermes Trismegistos himself was attributed the statement: 'What is above is like that which is below, and what is below is like that which is above, to effect a wonderful work'. That last clause implies that knowledge of how cosmic and terrestrial phenomena relate and interact confers a power to control or beneficially use those interactions.

Astrology was one of the many practical ramifications of this Hermetic principle of correspondences, but as with alchemy the ostensible meaning and purpose of the science resulted in its being widely misconceived, considered as a divinatory or predictive system based on a fatalistic philosophy. The misconception arises from the failure to understand that the above/below correspondences must be construed as correlated with correspondences between 'without' and 'within', or between the outer world of nature and the cosmos and the inner world of the human psyche.

Modern astrologers, who answer critics with the argument that they furnish clients with 'maps of consciousness' which enable them to fulfil inherent potentials, are using secular terms to describe the same project. As the Gnostics of old all knew and taught, however the soul's aspiration and journey may be represented in myth, ritual or spiritual discipline, it is essentially the inner journey that leads to the *gnosis*, to the only ultimately worthwhile knowledge and the only true liberation.

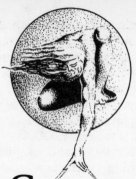

7 · THE GNOSTIC REVIVAL

The enlightenment sought by the Gnostics had little in common with the objectives of the philosophers of the eighteenth century Enlightenment, although those philosophers themselves often represented the Gnostics in favourable terms. In Voltaire's tale, *Candide*, the optimistic view of the eponymous hero's mentor, Panurge, that 'all is for the best in this best of possible worlds', is mocked by a narrative that recounts a succession of disasters, reversals of fortune and horrors that befall all its protagonists. The only realist among them, an old travelling scholar named Martin, tells Candide that he is a Manichaean, and to Candide's objection that there are no longer any Manichaeans in the world he replies: 'I can't help it; I can't think otherwise'. Candide exclaims, 'You must have the devil in you', to which Martin answers, 'The devil is so involved in the affairs of this world that he may well be in me, as he is everywhere else; but when I consider this globe, or rather this globule, I think that God must have abandoned it to some evil being'.

The 'best of possible worlds' idea is also mocked in Voltaire's short story, *Plato's Dream*, which shows his acquaintance with gnostic mythology. It tells how 'the great Demiurge, the eternal Geometer, having peopled the infinite spaces of the innumerable worlds, wanted to test the powers of the beings who had witnessed his work'. He gave each of them a piece of matter to work with, and to the being Démogorgon fell the lot of 'the bit of

96

mud that is called earth'. He fashioned it 'in the manner that we see it today', and thinking that he had accomplished a marvel expected the praise of his peers. But the other eternal beings only laughed and mocked his incompetence, particularly in creating man with 'so many passions and so little wisdom'. Démogorgon challenges them to do better and each of them creates a world (the planets of the solar system). The 'eternal Demiurge' puts a stop to their bickering as to whose work is the best by telling them that because they are themselves imperfect thay have all produced imperfect creations, and although they may learn and do better in future none will ever match the perfection of his own creation.

Voltaire's tales are *jeux d'esprit*, philosophical squibs concocted to shock and mock the religious and philosophical orthodoxies of his day. The Gnostics and their views served him as a whip to crack over the heads of believers in what were to him manifest falsehoods.

By no means was Voltaire, or any other philosopher of the Enlightenment, a Gnostic, but he and others of the movement opened the way to a sympathetic reappraisal of the countertradition that, in the field of literature at least, consolidated into a body of work of enduring quality that could be said to constitute a Gnostic revival.

WILLIAM BLAKE

If the poet William Blake was a beneficiary of the Enlightenment he showed scant appreciation of the fact. In his view the 'light of reason' had illuminated only the counterfeit reality of the material world. 'Mock on Mock on Voltaire Rousseau / Mock on Mock on 'tis all in vain' he wrote. His other *bête noir* was Newton, because he had demonstrated the mathematical symmetry of the movements of the planets.

Blake is a unique figure in English literature, not least for being one of its best known and worst understood poets. Every schoolchild used to know the first two lines of his poem *The Tyger*, but few ever understood the meaning of the second couplet: 'What immortal hand or eye / Dare frame thy fearful symmetry?' The answer is the Demiurge, Voltaire's 'eternal Geometer', the 'Great Artificer' of the Gnostics, the deity represented in Blake's other well-known work, the engraving 'The Ancient of Days', seen reaching down from the heavens and using geometrical instruments to create the world. 'Nature is the work of the Devil', Blake said in conversation with a friend, and we have to understand that for him Nature comprised the whole of creation, Newton's mechanical and ordered cosmos as well as the awesome 'tyger'.

Blake was a religious poet, and in his way a Christian, but his Christianity was radically different from that of the Orthodox Church. As he wrote in his late fragmentary poem, *The Everlasting Gospel*:

> The Vision of Christ that thou dost see
> Is my Vision's greatest enemy . . .
> Thine loves the same world that mine hates
> Thy Heaven doors are my Hell gates

He maintained that Orthodox interpretations of the scriptures were biased to support an ecclesiastical order that was non-spiritual and anti-life, and which reduced religion to mere virtue and morality:

> The Moral Christian is the Cause
> Of the Unbeliever and his Laws . . .
> For what is Antichrist but those
> Who against sinners Heaven close?[1]

Blake's major poetry was virtually unintelligible to his con-temporaries. His lyrics and *Songs of Innocence and Experi-ence* had their admirers, among them Wordsworth, but his long poems and 'Prophetic Books', which were printed in small editions illustrated by the poet's own engravings, had few readers and even fewer admirers. The problem was that the mythology, imagery and ideas expressed in the poems were pure Gnosticism.

Although he was self-educated Blake was deeply and widely read, and in the typical manner of the autodidact he was drawn to the discovery and study of ideas and works suppressed by or excluded from the prevailing culture. He sometimes said that the poems were 'dictated' to him, but however spontaneously they may have been written they welled up from a subconscious furnished with extensive knowledge of esoteric literature and traditions.

Like the Gnostics of old, Blake enjoyed being outrageous and perverse to shock the pious and complacent. Many of the 'Proverbs of Hell' in his early prose work, *The Marriage of Heaven and Hell*, were mischievously subversive. For instance:

> The road of excess leads to the palace of wisdom

> Prisons are built with stones of Law, Brothels
> with bricks of Religion

> As the caterpillar chooses the fairest leaves to
> lay her eggs on, so the priest lays his curse
> on the fairest joys

The central gnostic concept of the world as an inferior creation and the soul's prison is also suggested:

> The Giants who formed this world into its sensual exist-
> ence and now seem to live in it in chains, are in truth
> the cause of its life and the sources of all activity.[1]

In an earlier age the stake would have been the fate of a writer who dared utter such blasphemies. Blake suffered only neglect and poverty, but thanks to his skill as an artist and engraver he managed to maintain the independence to write his great gnostic works. These were a series of long poems, written between 1793 and 1815, beginning with *The Book of Urizen* and concluding with *Jerusalem*, with the longest poem, *Vala, or the Four Zoas*, falling into the middle period.

As the titles suggest, these poems develop a totally original mythology, at least in the sense that its protagonists have hitherto unheard-of names. The mythology itself is Blake's version of the cosmic drama of the Creation and Fall, and expounds distinctly gnostic ideas.

Consider the opening lines of *Jerusalem*:

> There is a Void, outside of Existence, which
> if entered into
> Englobes itself and becomes a Womb, such was
> Albions Couch
> A pleasant Shadow of Repose called Albions
> lovely land.

It requires knowledge of the gnostic tradition to conceive of Blake's 'Void, outside of Existence', but this is of course the 'realm beyond Being' in which the highest God existed before the cosmic drama began.

In Blake's mythology the God beyond Being was a composite of Eternals, the Divine Family, of which the Divine Man (Albion) and the Christ, or Jesus, were members. This composite was held together as a unity by Divine Energy, but in Man this energy waned; he fell into a sleep or passive state, and four aspects of his being that Blake calls his Zoas, which had formerly been integrated, became separated and independent and conflicted both with each other and with Man. This separation and its consequent conflicts was at once the fall of Man and the origin of creation.

The names of the four Zoas are: Urizen (Reason), Luvah (Passion), Tharmas (Sensation), and Urthona (Instinct). Each of these has a female counterpart that formerly existed in harmonious unity with the male but in the fallen state is frequently in conflict with him. With these divisions the scene is set for the development of a complex drama, which in typical gnostic manner combines and correlates cosmic, philosophical, religious and psychological significances.

In The Book of Urizen the titular deity, the God of Reason, creator of the material universe, boasts:

> I alone, even I, the winds merciless
> Bound; but condensing, in torrents
> They fall and fall; strong I repelled
> The vast waves, and arose on the waters
> A wide world of solid obstruction.

The last line expresses typical gnostic repugnance towards the material world. In the poem Urizen becomes fettered within his own creation in a body fashioned for him by his son Los. His fallen state is represented in typical gnostic imagery:

> Forgetfulness, dumbness, necessity!
> In chains of the mind locked up,
> Like fetters of ice shrinking together
> Disorganized, rent from Eternity ...
> The Immortal endured his chains,
> Tho' bound in a deadly sleep.
> All the myriads of Eternity,
> All the wisdom and joy of life,
> Roll like a sea around him,
> Except what his little orbs
> Of sight by degrees unfold.
> And now his eternal life
> Like a dream was obliterated.

Pathetic and deficient though he is, Urizen continues with his work of creation:

> He form'd a line and a plummet
> To divide the Abyss beneath
> He form'd a dividing rule
> He form'd golden compasses
> And began to explore the Abyss
> And he planted a garden of fruits.

The last line relates Urizen to the God of the *Genesis* creation myth. Blake does not, however, go on to satirise or re-interpret the Biblical story, but concludes his poem by accounting for the appearance of human beings within creation as an aberration. It would be difficult to find in literature a bleaker view of human life than his:

> Six days they shrunk up from existence
> And on the seventh day they rested
> And they bless'd the seventh day, in sick hope:
> And forgot their eternal life ...
> No more could they rise at will
> In the infinite void, but bound down
> To earth by their narrowing perceptions
> They lived a period of years

> Then left a noisom body
> To the jaws of devouring darkness
> And their children wept and built
> Tombs in the desolate places,
> And form'd laws of prudence, and call'd them
> The eternal laws of God.[1]

Here is gnostic nihilism in the extreme, but Blake was not fundamentally or ultimately a nihilist. Even from these lines it can be inferred that man has the potential for spiritual growth and liberation; it is the narrowness of his perceptions that keeps him in bondage. Only cleanse 'the doors of perception', wrote Blake, and 'everything will appear as it is, infinite'. The reason for his vehement hatred of religion and rationalist science was their conspiracy to limit and narrow perception, masquerading tendentious philosophical and moral principles as absolute truths. In *Jerusalem* he stated what he considered to be his 'great task':

> To open the Eternal Worlds, to open the
> immortal Eyes
> Of Man inwards into the Worlds of Thought;
> Into Eternity
> Ever expanding in the Bosom of God, the
> Human Imagination.[1]

Any of the great gnostic teachers of old might have described his aims in similar terms; it is the task of awakening the soul and guiding it towards *gnosis* and liberation. Note that the Eternal Worlds are within and that the spiritual journey towards union with the divine is pursued in the human imagination. Blake's poems are keys to *gnosis*, marvellous creations of a human imagination that had accomplished the spiritual journey and forged a language and mythology to help others to do so.

Blake was the most thoroughgoing Gnostic of the early Romantic movement; to the extent that he is not generally regarded as one of its typical or central figures. His work was too idiosyncratic and too specifically religious to be easily accommodated in a movement which, when it was not expressly atheist, as in Shelley and Byron, embraced a quasi-religious nature mysticism, as in Wordsworth and Coleridge. There were, however, many aspects of Romanticism itself that had a distinctly gnostic flavour; there was the cult of the Sublime, and the corresponding disdain for the mundane world, the 'divine discontent' with life and aspiration to transcend the ordinary human condition, whether by way of the transports of Genius or by welcoming 'easeful death' as the occasion of entry into a more glorious Beyond. There was the glorification of the unfettered human imagination and will, the repudiation of authority, the conviction that Genius neither could nor should brook any imposed restraints, which could be taken as licence to write the *Cent Jours de Sodom* or the *Fleurs du Mal*, or, by people less gifted than the Marquis de Sade and Baudelaire, as a licence for libertinage or even crime.

One of the central themes of Romantic literature is transgression, its proximate consequences and its ultimate resolution; which, as we have seen, is also one of the definitive subjects of gnostic literature.

GOETHE

This is the theme of Goethe's *Faust*. The story of the medieval scholar-magus who, weary and impatient with the constraints and ordinary satisfactions of life, conjures the Devil and pledges to serve him in the afterlife in exchange for a reciprocal service in the present, had been told before, notably in English by Shakespeare's contemporary Christopher Marlowe, but always with a conclusion conforming with Christian morality in which the transgressor suffers the just retribution of eternal damnation.

Goethe's two-part drama spurns conventional piety and recounts the legend from a more Romantic and more gnostic point of view.

Faust's discontent is both carnal and spiritual and is aggravated by the conflict between the two. He declares:

103

> Two souls, alas, are dwelling in my breast,
> And one is striving to foresake its brother.
> Unto the world in grossly loving zest,
> With clinging tendrils, one adheres;
> The other rises forcibly in quest
> Of rarefied ancestral spheres.[4]

This is the gnostic dualistic view of man as constituted of two irreconcilable elements. Conventional religion acknowledges a similar dualism, but replaces the gnostic emphasis on the incompatibility of the two elements with a schedule of observances and rituals designed to maintain them in a state of rather uneasy equilibrium until they are separated by death. The characteristic gnostic alternatives are to suppress and conquer the gross element by a life of rigorous asceticism, or to expunge it through indulgence and excess. Faust opts for the latter way, like the Carpocratians, who, according to Irenaeus, sought to release the soul from the cycle of birth and death in one lifetime by cramming every possible act and experience into it.

When Mephistopheles invites him to solicit any pleasure he wishes, Faust asserts a more exalted aspiration:

> I have no thought of joy.
> The reeling whirl I seek, the most painful excess,
> Enamoured hate and quickening distress.
> Cured of the craving to know all, my mind
> Shall not henceforth be closed to any pain,
> And what is apportioned out to all mankind,
> I shall enjoy deep in myself, contain
> Within my spirit summit and abyss,
> Pile on my breast their agony and bliss.[4]

This gnostic-Romantic programme of self-mortification and self-transcendence through excess only draws Mephisto's scorn; for he is the very Devil, and his objective is to entangle the soul more deeply in the morass of the lower world rather than facilitate its escape from it. He resorts to the characteristic devilish stratagem of drugging Faust with a potion that suppresses his higher aspirations and replaces them with a raging lust for the first woman he sets eyes on. Mephisto gleefully aids and abets Faust's seduction of the young virgin, Gretchen, to the point of furnishing the infatuated girl with a sleeping draught to give to her mother so that Faust can spend the night with her. She subsequently suffers a fate reminiscent of the Valentinian Sophia or Simon Magus's Helena: pregnant, bereaved of her mother (apparently poisoned by Mephisto's drug) and her brother (killed by Faust with Mephisto's help when he sought to avenge her), humiliated and dubbed a harlot, and finally imprisoned in a dungeon and condemned to death. Faust, forced to flee after the murder but repentant of the tragic consequences of his lust and inadvertence, seeks forgetfulness by accompanying Mephisto to the witches' and wizards' revel, the Walpurgis Night. His participation in this orgy of sensuality, licence and buffoonery is a cathartic immersion in the dark realms of the debauched world and his own psyche, from which he emerges resolved to rescue Gretchen. Mephisto fulfils his service pact by facilitating Faust's access to the dungeon by drugging the jailor, but for all Faust's pleading Gretchen refuses a salvation effected by the Devil's powers.

Thus ends Part One of the tragedy, which was published in 1808. It was not until after Goethe's death in 1832 that Part Two appeared. Shorter, more metaphysical, less dramatic in the sense of developing its theme through theatrical incident, Part Two is a very different work; by no means a sequel or afterthought as it resolves questions that were left unanswered in Part One. It is only when the two Parts are taken together that it becomes clear that *Faust* is a cosmic drama, with close affinities with the gnostic cosmic drama of the soul's fall into chaos and eventual liberation and restitution. The theme is announced at the beginning of Part One, in the 'Prologue in Heaven', when Mephistopheles wagers with God that he can prevail upon Faust to surrender his soul to him for eternity. God accepts the wager, expressing his conviction that however abysmally the soul may err, 'A good man in his darkling aspiration / Remembers the right road throughout his quest'. The end of Part One saw Faust repentant and distressed, but at the beginning of Part Two he has, without realising it, reverted to being Mephisto's creature. He has accumulated immense wealth and property, sanctioning robbery and coercion to do so. When eventually he dies it would appear that Mephisto has won his wager, but the company of devils who appear to carry off his soul are opposed by a host of angels who use the stratagem of the Messenger in the Manichaean myth, manifesting as lovely youths who distract Mephisto and the devils by arousing their lust, and thereby succeed in rescuing Faust's soul and carrying it off to the realm of Light. In a final scene we learn that he was ultimately saved by the intercession of the spirit of Gretchen, who, like Sophia in the *Pistis Sophia*, had herself regained the realm of Light through her devotion and penitence.

Like Blake, Goethe excoriated and satirised the Church. When he was accused of having written a pagan work he replied mischievously: 'I, pagan? Well, I let Gretchen be executed; what do people want that could be more Christian?' How familiar he was with gnostic literature must be a matter of conjecture, although the correspondence with the Manichaean myth mentioned above does suggest some familiarity. To seek to co-opt him to the ranks of the fully-fledged Gnostics would be to overstate the case, but certainly in writing *Faust* he both drew upon the tradition and contributed to it.

MELVILLE

Hermann Melville did the same with his great novel, *Moby Dick*. When he had finished it Melville wrote to his friend, the novelist Nathaniel Hawthorne, 'I have written a wicked book, and feel as innocent as the lamb'. He also referred to it as a 'book of secrets'.

In typical gnostic manner, Melville employed allegory, ambiguity and irony to both reveal and conceal his meaning. The novel is a strange amalgamation of realism and symbolism, of adventure yarn and metaphysical allegory. It contains long passages of factual information about the whale and about the methods, the economics and the hazards of the whaling industry in the mid-nineteenth century. Ostensibly it is a straight story of a whaling expedition, and although the whaler's captain has an obsession with pursuing a particular whale, the monstrous white Moby Dick, this is explained by a previous encounter with the creature in which he was grievously injured and lost a leg. There is nothing 'wicked' about any of this. It is wholesome material, fit for making into an action movie or abridging into an enthralling adventure tale for schoolboys. The novel has suffered both fates, though one wonders what schoolboys made of Captain Ahab's language, which is more Old Testament than old sea-dog.

The language, like Melville's other literary devices, occludes the book's 'secrets'. Many readers will agree with the verdict of the First Mate, the pious and rational Starbuck, that Ahab is mad, and will regard this as confirmed by the captain's agreement that he is 'madness maddened' and 'demoniacal'. His vehement harangue addressed to the creator in the final pages appears not only mad but also blasphemous:

> Thou knowest not how came ye, hence callest thyself unbegotten: certainly knowest not thy beginning, hence callest thyself unbegun. I know that of me, which thou knowest not of thyself, oh, thou omnipotent. There is some unsuffusing thing beyond thee to whom all thy eternity is but time, all thy creativeness mechanical.

Yes, this creator god is the inferior, ignorant, arrogant and malevolent deity that the Gnostics always mocked and reviled, and the white whale, Moby Dick, is his creature. Ahab's 'madness maddened' is the sanity of a man who has apprehended that nature, the world, and their creator are all counterfeit, who refuses to acquiesce to their power, and who, in the name of humanity, mounts an heroic, if ultimately futile, revolt against them. 'An inscrutable malice is chiefly what I hate,' says Ahab, 'and be the white whale agent, or be the white whale principal, I will wreak that hate upon him. Talk not to me of blasphemy, man'.

The 'wickedness' of *Moby Dick* consists in its expressing, powerfully if covertly, the gnostic philosophy. Melville felt 'innocent as the lamb' because he wholeheartedly embraced that philosophy. He was acquainted with at least some of the old gnostic literature and, typically for a Gnostic, was not above doing a bit of counterfeiting himself. He wrote a short poem which he titled *Fragments of a Lost Gnostic Poem*, containing the lines: 'Matter in the end will never abate / His ancient brutal claim'.

At the end of *Moby Dick* the whale has destroyed the boat, *The Pequod*, and all aboard her have perished except Ishmael, the book's narrator, who explains the psychology of Ahab's obsession, saying that he had transferred the idea of 'that intangible malignity which has been from the beginning, which the ancient Ophites of the east reverenced . . . to the abhorred white whale'. (The Ophites were a minor gnostic sect.) *Moby Dick* may be a 'book of secrets' and covert meanings, but when it is read with understanding there can be no doubt about the fact that it is one of the great gnostic texts of modern literature.

The whaler's name, *The Pequod*, means 'orphan', and in the final paragraph Ishmael ruefully reflects upon his own situation as that of the orphan. There are covert meanings here, too: the orphan, the abandoned, the cast out. Ishmael survives, clinging to a bit of wreckage in the middle of a vast, indifferent ocean.

Moby Dick also lends itself to an Existentialist interpretation, but Existentialism was itself a kind of secular Gnosticism; a Gnosticism divested of its conviction that through knowledge and effort man can ultimately transcend his wretched earthly condition. It represented the human situation as being thrown into existence in an alien world, unable to derive any sense of meaning or purpose either from that world or from any transcendent order. A scrap of human flotsam clinging to wreckage in the middle of a hostile ocean is an apt image of the Existentialist view of man.

EXISTENTIALISM

Existentialism developed in the nineteenth century, in the work of the Danish philosopher Søren Kierkegaard and later the German, Friedrich Nietzsche, but its origins go back to the previous century and the French writer Blaise Pascal.

It was Pascal who first expressed the implications of the Copernican cosmology; the realization that the earth was not the centre of the universe but merely 'a remote corner of nature', and that the infinite spaces of the universe were ignorant of and indifferent to the existence of the 'thinking reed', man. Pascal advocated belief in God as a rational 'wager' since there was nothing to lose from being wrong, and professed a firm belief himself, but he did not believe that God was inherent in the world or that any divine attributes could be inferred from the order of the cosmos or from nature. Kierkegaard, too, was a believer, but he rejected the orthodox doctrine concerning the relation of man to God. He insisted on the inscrutability of divine purposes, the separateness of man and God. Man is 'his own project', not God's; he finds himself in the world, compelled to act and to choose, and through his acts and choices he makes and defines his essential self. If he wants meaning and purpose he must create them for himself, and cannot look to God for either guidance or approval.

Nietzsche went further than Pascal and Kierkegaard by asserting categorically that 'God is dead', a statement which he enlarged upon as meaning that 'we have not the slightest justification for positing a beyond, or an "in itself" of things, which is "divine", which is morality in person'.[6] It followed, he argued, that all values were devalued, there was no ordained order of values or morality, and consequently 'everything is permitted'.

The consequences of this Nietzschean nihilism were subsequently explored in numerous literary works, most notably in the novels of Dostoevski and Hermann Hesse. It went further than the gnostic nihilism which held that the god of this world could command neither man's respect nor his obedience, but its consequences were the same.

Existentialists, like the Gnostics, tended to regard the material, physical world, with repugnance, as constituting a mode of being utterly different from and inimical to the mode appropriate for man. The most celebrated Existentialist of the present century, the French philosopher Jean-Paul

109

Sartre, developed a distinction made by Martin Heidegger between two modes of being; being-in-itself (*être-en-soi*) and being-for-itself (*être-pour-soi*). The former is the mode of being of things, of nature; and the latter is, or should be, the mode of human beings, although it rarely is because human beings generally relinquish the freedom that is a fundamental and unique attribute of their being and acquiesce in a mode of existence appropriate only for things; the vegetative mode as Blake would have called it. The title of Sartre's novel, *Nausea*, expresses the feeling that its hero experiences when he contemplates either nature or other human beings in their unaware and materialist existence. Although there is no suggestion that the man-nature dichotomy and man's being a 'stranger' in the material world is attributable to the existence in him of any 'divine spark', Existentialism endorses the fundamentally gnostic view of the human condition as one of entrapment in an 'inauthentic' mode of existence, and that to escape from the trap demands a sustained mental effort of awareness, a definitive choice of the freedom that is the uniquely human attribute and a relentless revolt against the forces that would constrain it. Otherwise, as Sartre's hero puts it, 'man is a useless passion'.

What are we to make of these similarities? No existentialist ever acknowledged Gnosticism as a source or influence, and there is no question of the conscious perpetuation of a tradition. When correspondences manifest between things distantly separated, does it not suggest that there are other, maybe profounder, reasons than influence or derivation? The German historian and philosopher Oswald Spengler pointed out parallels between our century and the first centuries of the Christian era, maintaining that they were identical phases in the life cycle of their cultures and could even be said to be 'contemporaneous'. Do the Gnostics speak to us across the centuries so familiarly because we are their contemporaries in this sense? Is there a *Zeitgeist*, a 'spirit of the age', that manifests in a convergence of ideas, themes and preoccupations in philosophical, literary and other creative areas? If so, might it not have close parallels with and engender similar works as the *Zeitgeist* of an earlier age?

The Existentialists may not have been aware of the gnostic connection and tradition but there have been other writers in the present century who certainly were.

W.B. Yeats was deeply read in esoteric literature and many of the poems he wrote in the 1920s and '30s express gnostic ideas in powerful and sometimes terrible imagery. (As in the last lines of The Second Coming: 'And what rough beast, its hour come round at last / Slouches towards Bethlehem to be born?') Some of the novels of Hermann Hesse have gnostic themes and characters who speak explicitly and sympathetically about the Gnostics (notably Demian, and also Narziss and Goldmund and The Steppenwolf). More recently Lawrence Durrell introduced gnostic themes into his novels, not only in The Alexandria Quartet, where the action is located in the ancient city of the Gnostics, but also in his later novel, Monsieur, in which a modern gnostic teacher, Akkad, expounds the philosophy at length. Numerous other examples could be cited, and the subject of the gnostic revival in late Romanticism would make a book in itself, but we must press on to conclude with a consideration of the man who not only wrote the most profound modern gnostic work, but also taught us to understand that the reasons for Gnosticism's enduring appeal go deeper than an intellectual assent to its philosophy or a response to its revolt against and contradiction of the dominant Western cultural tradition, and that they reside in the fact that its ideas and images arise directly from and speak directly to the unconscious.

CARL JUNG

Carl Jung wrote the Seven Sermons to the Dead in three evenings some time at the beginning of 1917 and subsequently published the work in a small edition for the perusal of friends only. This was relatively early in his career and he clearly did not want the publication of this short, poetical and mystical treatise to compromise his reputation as a psychologist, physician and scientist. Not until his autobiography was posthumously published (in 1962) was it revealed that the

111

Seven Sermons, together with other mystical writings from the same period which were not published, were the fount of all his creativity, and that all that he accomplished in his later work was already contained in them. He also revealed in his autobiography that the composition of the *Seven Sermons* was accompanied by the occurrence of supernatural events in his home, events that today parapsychologists would call poltergeist phenomena. Members of his family as well as he were aware of oppressive presences in the house, and when Jung exclaimed, 'For God's sake, what in the world is this?' he received an answer from a chorus of voices: 'We have come back from Jerusalem where we found not what we sought'. These are the words with which the *Seven Sermons to the Dead* opens.

As noted earlier, Jung attributed their authorship to Basilides of Alexandria. Alexandria, the city of the gnosis, and Jerusalem, the city of the Judaeo-Christian God, the oppressive law-giver, are thus opposed.

The dead, who have not found what they sought in Jerusalem, are beings who have not achieved gnosis. Each of the Sermons opens with an urgent and clamorous demand from them for knowledge and understanding, and 'Basilides' sets forth his teaching in allusive, condensed, sometimes poetic and sometimes discursive sentences. 'The dead' are not the spirits of the deceased, they are the living dead, they are ourselves in so far as we are without gnosis. The *Seven Sermons* reveal, to those who understand and can apply the knowledge they convey, the way to transcend death, to still the clamour of the soul tormented by its inherent contradictions and confused understanding.

Jung the psychologist referred to the attainment of gnosis, of psychic wholeness, as 'Individuation'. 'Basilides' introduces the term in the first Sermon. The Pleroma, he teaches, is at once emptiness and fullness, nothing and everything, nowhere and everywhere, devoid of qualities yet containing all qualities. The created world is separate from the Pleroma although the Pleroma penetrates it everywhere as sunlight penetrates the air. The created world is the differentiated world, as distinct from the world of sameness of the Pleroma. Man discriminates

112

qualities in the Pleroma which are really projections from his own being. Differentiations between light and dark, energy and matter, time and space, good and evil, the beautiful and the ugly, and so forth, are cancelled out in the Pleroma, but in human beings they are active:

> We die to the extent that we fail to discriminate. For this reason the natural impulse of the created being is directed toward differentiation and toward the struggle against the ancient, pernicious state of sameness. The natural tendency is called *Principium Individuationis* (Principle of Individuation). This principle is indeed the essence of every created being.[5]

We are the victims of the conflicts between these pairs of opposites. 'In us the Pleroma is rent in two.' People strive to resolve this state of division by pursuing, for instance, exclusively the good and the beautiful. When they do so they are not being true to their nature, which is differentiation, and the inevitable result is that they attain also the evil and the ugly. The only way out of this dilemma is to learn to differentiate ourselves from the contraries. 'If we know how to know ourselves as being apart from the pairs of opposites, then we have attained to salvation'. This is the goal of the process of Individuation. It is not attained by seeking or rejecting any of the opposites, but by enabling them to become resolved through their interaction and maintaining the self apart from them, which means not being governed by thoughts and ideas 'because thinking alienates us from our true nature'. Therefore, says 'Basilides', 'I must teach knowledge to you'.

This is Jungian psychology in a nutshell. He later formulated it in the principle that every dynamic component of the psyche has its 'shadow', and that if we allow our consciousness to prescribe for us a one-sided attitude or course of action the 'shadow' will be active in the unconscious and eventually assert itself to subvert our efforts. In the created world, 'Basilides' goes on to explain in the second Sermon, differentiation manifests supremely in the co-existence of God and Devil, whose distinguishing counteracting principles are 'fullness and emptiness, generation and destruction'. What these deities have in common is activity. Both are active in the world and in the psyche. To consider evil to be merely the absence of good is to deny the dynamic interactivity of these powerful forces, and results in the evil principle asserting itself all the more potently, as has been repeatedly experienced in the history of Western culture.

What must be understood is that above the Devil and the God of this world (whom 'Basilides' calls *Helios*, or the Sun) there is another deity, whom he calls Abraxas. 'If the Pleroma were capable of having a being', he says, 'Abraxas would be its manifestation.

> Abraxas is the god whom it is difficult to know. His power is the very greatest, because man does not perceive it at all. Man sees the *summum bonum* (supreme good) of the sun, and also the *infinum malum* (endless evil) of the devil, but Abraxas he does not see, for he is indefinable life itself, which is the mother of good and evil alike.

The third Sermon is devoted entirely to describing the awesome magnificence of the God-Devil 'about whom you know nothing, because men have forgotten him'. Abraxas is 'truly the terrible one'. He is

> the sun and also the eternally gaping abyss of emptiness . . . magnificent even as the lion at the very moment when he strikes his prey down. His beauty is like the beauty of a spring morn . . . He is the monster of the underworld . . . He is the brightest light of day and the deepest night of madness . . . He is the mightiest manifest being, and in him creation becomes frightened of itself. He is the revealed protest of creation against the Pleroma and its nothingness.[5]

And much more. 'Only a poet could understand', Jung told a friend, and the third Sermon is poetry of a high order, as must needs be to evoke the forgotten God in whom the powers of God-the-Sun and of the Devil are subsumed, who is 'undefinable life itself', the sheer energy that manifests when the contrary principles at work in the world and the psyche become *complementaries*. How is man to cope with Abraxas? 'Basilides' tells us: 'To see him means blindness; to know him is sickness; to worship him is death; to fear him is wisdom; not to resist him means liberation'. In other words there can be no attainment of *gnosis*, no Individuation, without submission to the imperatives of the raw energy of the life force, no matter what psychic turbulence and suffering the experience might entail.

'Basilides' teaching in the fourth and fifth Sermons turns to the multiplicity and diversity of the gods and devils that are active in the created world. 'Woe unto you', he tells 'the dead',

> for you have substituted the oneness of God for the diversity which cannot be resolved into one. Through this you have created the torment of incomprehension, and the mutilation of the created world, the essence and law of which is diversity. How can you be true to your nature when you attempt to make one out of many? What you do to the the gods, that also befalls you.[5]

This is not simply a repudiation of Judaeo-Christian monotheism. These innumerable gods are what Jung the psychologist called 'archetypes of the unconscious'. The definitive property of life is change, transformation, progressive integration, and Jung knew from his own experiences and his work with patients that the facilitators of this process are components of the unconscious that are activated by images and symbols, personifications, the beings and creatures of dreams, the gods and goddesses of myths. These powerful transformative archetypes have to be recognized, respected, allowed to do their work. As with Abraxas, 'to worship them is death', but 'not to resist them is liberation'.

There is not enough space in the present context to undertake summaries and commentaries on Sermons four to seven. Suffice it to say that they express and elucidate these symbols and indicate how, properly understood and used, they may help 'the dead' to awaken to gnosis, the disoriented and confused psyche to 'individuate' and attain wholeness.

Jung has been said to have been the last of the Gnostics. However, the verdict on the tradition has been pronounced before and has always proved to be premature, and it is largely to Carl Jung that we owe our understanding of why it will always be so.

BIBLIOGRAPHY AND NOTES

Reference numbers in the text refer to the following sources:

1. Blake, William, *The Complete Poems*, Penguin Books, London, 1977.
2. Churton, Tobias, *The Gnostics*, Weidenfeld, London, 1987.
3. Duvernoy, Jean, *La Religion des Cathares*, Edouard Privat, Toulouse, 1976 (extracts are author's translation).
4. Goethe, Johann Wolfgang von, *Faust* (tr. Walter Kaufmann), Anchor Books, New York, 1961.
5. Hoeller, Stephan A., *The Gnostic Jung*, Theosophical Publishing House, Wheaton, Illinois, 1982.
6. Jonas, Hans, *The Gnostic Religion*, Beacon Press, Boston, 1963.
7. Ladurie, Emmanuel Le Roy, *Montaillou*, Penguin Books, London, 1980.
8. Mead, G.R.S., *Fragments of a Faith Forgotten*, University Books, New York, 1960.
9. Pagels, Elaine, *The Gnostic Gospels*, Weidenfeld, London, 1979.
10. Robinson, James (editor), *The Nag Hammadi Library*, Harper, San Francisco, 1988.

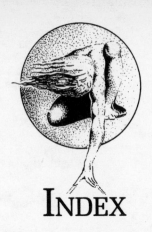

INDEX